HAVE YOU STOPPED GROWING?

RAJENDRA CHANDORKAR

Copyright © Rajendra Chandorkar
All Rights Reserved.

This book has been published with all efforts taken to make the material error-free after the consent of the author. However, the author and the publisher do not assume and hereby disclaim any liability to any party for any loss, damage, or disruption caused by errors or omissions, whether such errors or omissions result from negligence, accident, or any other cause.

While every effort has been made to avoid any mistake or omission, this publication is being sold on the condition and understanding that neither the author nor the publishers or printers would be liable in any manner to any person by reason of any mistake or omission in this publication or for any action taken or omitted to be taken or advice rendered or accepted on the basis of this work. For any defect in printing or binding the publishers will be liable only to replace the defective copy by another copy of this work then available.

DEDICATED TO

ALL WHO

LOVE THEIR COUNTRY

Contents

Acknowledgements

It gives me a great pleasure when I write this page of my book. It is very reassuring to know that in this age of cutthroat competition, there are so many people, who are ready to offer help to me.

The constructive criticism from my friends, those who read the manuscript and found time to discuss with me, suggest improvements, has been a sort of a test market for this book.

A special thanks for Dr. Avdhesh Shukla, and Mr. Pratap Shukla who are patiently helping me out of my digital issues. With them around world seems easy.

Sudipta, my wife, is always around when I need a word of support and encouragement. Soumitra, my son is the first and foremost critic and keeps on contributing the new generation angle.

Rajendra Chandorkar

Foreword

During my school days, I never felt embarrassed when I said, 'I love my country'.

People around me accepted the feelings of patriotism and honesty without any apparent pinch of salt. Somethings changed, somewhere in the later years, when people started scoffing at such an expression. The unexpected, unabashed shamelessness displayed by the 'Neta's'*, (mind you, not the leaders, Leaders are different than Netas), the extent of corruption on moral, ethical, organizational and of course financial levels, could never allow any normal Indian, to believe that good old values like, integrity, honesty, patriotism were alive and would remain alive. On this backdrop when you start to venture into the period of 2000 AD, and after, you shall feel that the Indian Polity has apparently lost its soul, somewhere.

The common Indian feels helpless and disillusioned as the officials who are supposed to protect, along with the Netas, instead of protecting the law, the economic order, are definitely involved in perpetual spoiling the functioning of the system.

The basic values are in doubt; the punishments to the people who break the law are non-existent. More often than not, you know that your "Neta" is a corrupt, a criminal and a lopsided individual and yet you find that wins the polling contest, by employing methods that are uniquely unwarranted and disgusting.

That the leaders are supposed to serve the suffering common man is forgotten long back. The leaders like Gandhi, Tilak are only remembered as a professional hazard, that too only on 15th August or 26th January while the loot, the plundering of the country goes on. The terms sacrifice, moral posture, dignity, dignity of labor and the protocol are all thrown out of windows and the sole reason for the Neta to join politics is "To make money and make more money".

*(*Neta is an Indian version of modern political leader mostly immoral version.)*

The insecurity doled out by the present circumstances is the major reason for the unrest, uneasy calm that prevails in once a very peaceful country. Every tangle, which could have been sorted out, has been move often than not kept alive, fuelling or dousing, as per the 'needs' of the Netas. The basic belief, the basic comfort has been rocked by such lousy people, who tend to hold the country for a ransom. The misfortune of the present-day Indian is such that he cannot be sure about any person, whether he should trust or not? How such a situation has been able to continue over last few decades? Whatever was sacred has been spoilt. Whatever is good for the nation has been seemingly dumped. The vulgar antics of the third-rate politicians have been highlighted by the media, the newspapers. Such a situation has proved a great inhibitor in the overall growth of our country. It contributes negatively as it just kills the initiative of common man.

I suddenly realized that this is not what my country should be. This is not he same nation for which so many have and had supremely sacrificed. The country, in the dreams of all the freedom fighters, poets, was quite different from what we find it today. I wish to implore all those Indians, who love their country to start thinking in a positive way, to start working towards developing a resilient India, which should be so strong intrinsically, that all the artificial jolts, may not disturb the serenity and prosperity of our beloved country. The book is one step, I hope, in a right direction. It should change the thinking, towards the betterment of an individual, an organization and of course, the nation. I sincerely believe that common Indians with a correct moral and ethical base shall emerge as the **strongest single component** towards building a strong and powerful nation. The sooner the process starts, better are the chances of the success.

***

Preface

To The Reader

"Have You Stopped Growing?"

What is your first and actual response to the above question? You, may be, are able to answer, this very rarely asked question, at this very instant or, as usual, you many say that it would take some time, before you can. I shall share my experience with you. I was on a sales tour, and as a part of the same, I was waiting, for a train on a railway platform. I am interested in everything around me, and I spotted two persons, from selling activity. Obviously, one was a supervisor and the other, a frontline salesman. The pair was discussing about recent visits to their customers and probably, because of some unprecedented huge order, they were both in an elated mood. Probably their targets were met and hence they seemed to relax. By then, I was very interested in them, because they were unknowingly stepping into an area called as "inactive zone". What they would have, then, decided was very interesting. Suddenly, the mobile of supervisor rang, and when he picked up the call, from his response, very obviously it was from his Big Boss fro headquarters. As a result of this call, they stopped talking about their recent achievement, and once more concentrated on the future. They started talking about their plans for the city they were supposed to visit, and planned for getting positive results. I really had no way of knowing as to what the mobile call said to the supervisor, but then out of sheer curiosity, I approached to supervisor and after the introductions etc., I asked him about what his Boss had said. The supervisor was very surprised and probably embarrassed also, but seeing that I also was from the same field he shared the following with me. He said that his boss was a though one and even though, he had said a work of appreciation, he reminded the need to work towards the next immediate and essential goal. As a result of this very important and may be **life changing** call, the supervisor was saved from entering the most destructive **"inactive zone."** The supervisor could, otherwise, would have basked in the glory of his recent achievement and very soon would have found out that there is nothing in the future to cheer about.

What about you? How often you have achieved something which makes you feel that you have been a **"success"**? How many miles you have to go down your memory lane for remembering the last time you experienced the glory of success? The longer the distance you travel in your memory lane, the surer is the clear indication that you have inadvertently stopped to grow.

I am amazed when I meet people who say "I have arrived". Further they claim that they have achieved what they are supposed to achieve. The feeling of having achieved is very worthwhile and it should be enjoyed, but for a very short period only. The sooner you realize, that you should set a fresh goal is better for your own esteem and posture. If you have decided that this is "how much" you are supposed to grow, that is "how much" you may grow, that too, if you are lucky. One moment of self-realisation shall tell you that if your stop your efforts to go ahead, that if you stop to visualize you next achievement level, you shall have **only one direction** to go and that is **downwards.**

I have seen many talented people to reach a certain competence level, and then gradually fade into a life of mediocrity. Mediocrity is a very potent virus, which can infect you in nay stage of life. The symptoms are very dreary and the result awful. You stop growing, or in simple language, you stop living.

I request you, my reader, to please read this book with a clear mind, try to analyze your potential, try to review your achievements, regroup yourself and decide what you want to do.

    ***

CHAPTER ONE

What Is Growth?

As is my habit, I put this question to quite a few people, from diverse backgrounds and occupations. They answered the question, and it was very natural that the emphasis was on their own activity, or way of life. Quite a few sincerely confessed that they were not ready for such question. After all "Growth is growth".

Growth means increase. An increment is growth. In alphabetical order if we try to find out what growth means then you shall come across following words.

- *Advancement
- Augmentation
- Broadening
- Cultivation
- Development
- Diversification
- Enlargement
- Evolution
- Extension
- Improvement
- Increase
- Maturation
- Multiplication
- Proliferation
- Prosperity
- Stretching
- Success
- Swelling
- Tumor

- Widening

*Webster's New Dictionary & Thesaurus

When you try to fit the process of growth in all the above references you should be surprised to see the capacity of this small word.

Usually, growth is associated with living organisms. When we talk of growth, we generally understand that it is with reference to the 'Living'. Is it true? A snowball, a cloud, a small spring getting larger in form of a river, a heap of papers, all grow, but are not living. Let us not forget, **garbage,** which has been a major challenge to all municipal corporations, all over the world. This point has been raised to remind you, that even, things which do not live also grow, to huge proportions.

Growth can be in form of increase in **number**, in form of **size**, in form of **capacity,** or **knowledge.** Political parties are worried about numbers, a doctor is worried about the size of tumor, an industrialist always talks about production capacity and volume of sales, a professor is worried about increase or decrease of knowledge, in the minds of students. **Everybody is wishing to grow in whatever field he sets himself in, then why it is so, that only a few of us can reach where we want to reach?**

After a lot of interaction, with a lot of people, I try to define growth. To me growth means following: -

1. **"Growth is a mechanism of automatic or intentional substitution of undesired old elements or habits or all such things, by new substitutes, in the journey of successful life."**
2. Growth is also increase in your own numbers to ensure that you are represented in the distant future, by you descendents. Those who are seen today should thank their forefathers, who fought against all odds about which nobody can even imagine. The beauty of the efforts to merely survive, put in by our ancestors is a matter of debate, conjecture and most importantly comprehension. What must be feelings of the pre-historic man when he first saw fire, flood, lightening, earthquake, volcanic eruption, avalanches, fierce and hunting animals, extreme temperatures, poisonous plants, and so many other mighty factors, which made living itself very arduous and difficult. But the "Man" survived, even though apparently not endowed with any special physical attributes. Most importantly, not only he survived but also managed to pass on the vital survival tips to his progeny and to this, we all owe our

existence today.

3. J. Krishnamurthy, the great thinker, simply says that "Growth is in the totality". I took some time before I could understand what the great mind has to say. The full implication of the statement can be interpreted by each individual in his own way, but to me it means that growth should be on a holistic scale. In isolation, any single parameter of growth loses value and significance.

4. Growth to me is the combination of following: -

- G - Get the flexible attitude
- R - Rise to the challenge
- O - Organise
- W - Welcome the winning ways
- T - Thrust forward
- H - Harness good habits

(G) Get the flexible attitude - Anything that is rigid resists growth. If you are rigid, you stop even listening to new ideas. As it is we have accepted today that attitude is foremost factor for possible success.

(R) Rise to the challenge – When you accept a new challenge, you work in different mood, and fashion. This alone can help you grow immensely. So volunteer for new challenges!

(O) Organize – To deliver correct action, it is imperative that you organise yourself, your activity, so that when you actually start working your plan, you do not waste time. First time, you plan in your mind, correctly imagining and outlining and then subsequently in actual conditions.

(W) Welcome the winning ways – Identify the winning ways, mark them and walk only on paths, which are proven.

(T) Thrust forward – Look ahead, reach there. Cut all the ropes which may bind you.

(H) Harness good habits – Good habits are scarce. If you have them, preserve them, make them grow. If you feel, you miss some of them; it is never late to try to cultivate such habits.

Growth is a natural process, so common, that most of us do not even think about it. The "beginning" and the "end" of all of us is pre-decided events. Whatever grows has to end sometime, somewhere. The beauty of the process is you ensure that whatever time you have you can decide what to do with it. When you are growing always remember that growth is marching towards the end, so it is better to manage your resources in such a way, that you achieve what you want, enjoy the same for a while and then, set new targets and goals.

   ***

CHAPTER TWO

Classification of Growth

To understand the process of growth, let us classify the process. Various types or areas, where you are supposed to grow can be detailed as below: -

- **Personal Growth**
- **Education Growth**
- **Social Growth**
- **Spiritual Growth**
- **Organisation Growth**

As you understand growth is with reference to yourself, you may add or deduct a few types, depending upon your analysis.

Personal Growth:

The growth of a person starts right from the day he or she is conceived. In the body of the mother, a fertilized egg goes through a cycle of cell divisions, in a very much predecided manner. All through the gestation period, the boy or a girl is developing in a general, as well as in a very... very specific way. At this stage, he or she is not exposed at all, to anything outside, but even at this stage, it absorbs influences. (These days the current "in-thing" is a load of CDs/Cassettes/DVDs/Online content, for the "mother and her child" in the belly. These inputs provide music, mantras from sanatan scriptures and so many other things which are expected to influence the child right there, in the uterus. The ancient Indians were aware of this and there have been many examples of such knowledge throughout our history and scriptures).

When the child is born, it still is very vulnerable, still fully dependent, for all his existence, on his mother. But its brain is working overtime. The transition from a warm and dark comfort zone inside the mother's body the child is exposed to the stark light and facts of the ensuing human life.

He does not know about his name, region, religion, which would bind him for his entire future life. It has so many things to see, to absorb knowledge from. Everything the child sees is an experience in itself. Smell, sight, fragrance, the touch, the sound of his mother or father and all other persons around him teach him some thing new. Each day is a new learning and it comes naturally. He understands the relationship between his crying and his getting fed. Most children are fortunate enough as they are loved, cared for, fussed over, by their parents grand-parents etc. But there are quite a few, who are abandoned by their parents, who grow up as orphans. How do they manage? As you start thinking about this, it becomes absolutely fascinating and you cannot but appreciate the ever existing and omnipotent blessings of the Almighty. Each individual of the billions of human beings grows to his given size and stature in a precisely predetermined pattern. The point here is that though every human-being is endowed with immense potential, intellect and emotional exclusive fingerprint, only a few do reach the pinnacle of success.

The personal growth of a person can be further divided into,

a. **<u>Physical growth</u>**
b. **<u>Mental or intellectual growth</u>**

a. **<u>Physical growth</u>** – This is an aspect of a growth over which the individual has hardly any control. He is born with the genes given to him by his parents, with predefined combination of dominant and recessive traits. A son of a tall father very rarely is dwarf. Why? Because of the genetics involved. For each and every character, there is a responsible gene, in its dominant or recessive expression. Children attend their predetermined height, weight, shape and form; say at 18 years of age. At this stage he is supposed to be fully grown. The person can achieve slight betterment in this, by regular exercise, neat and clean habits. Unless a person does something drastically wrong, he turns out to be a physically normal adult.

a. **<u>Mental or intellectual growth</u>** – The growth of person in the mental faculty can be very tricky as it has a variety of factors affecting. Please try to understand by following schematic representation: -

Schematic Representation of Age & Absorption of Knowledge

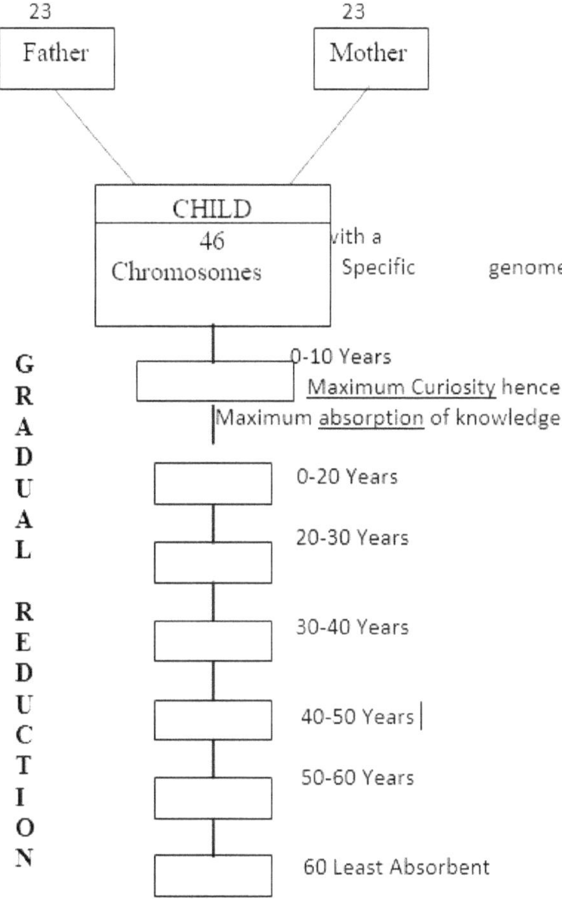

Age & Absorption

As soon as the child is conceived it has already received a **full quota of genetic information,** from his parents. It is very fascinating that this miniature format is to last for its entire life period, with minimal or no changes in the future life, creating physical and mental characteristics or traits as called by genetic scientist.

The physical attributes or traits can be very rarely affected by the surroundings, unless the surroundings include a continuous food shortage or exposure to extreme cold and severe conditions.

But the main differentiating factor, which separates a human being from his fellow humans, is his capacity to absorb information from his surroundings, further utilize it for his betterment and rise to the top, in presence of severe competition.

It is of common knowledge that children are curious, inquisitive and generally interested in anything around them, even if it does not concern them. I have yet to see a negative child. But as they absorb all influences, good or bad, useful or useless and hence in this part of his life phase, up to 10 years they are very active, very bold and generally happy.

Subsequently, from 10 years onwards up to 60 years, their areas of interests are gradually reduced, and they become less receptive to new ideas. Try convincing or selling a new idea, to a person in his or her late fifties and you shall certainly realise, what I am trying to say. This further worsens in cases of persons over and above 60. Conventionally, it is also accepted that a person is "grown up" at 50 years of age, but is it true? How a person – considered to be a grown-up adult – shows a distinct aversion to anything new? What I feel is that a person considered to be **grown up** is actually a person who has **stopped growing**, as he is not interested in anything new. So, in fact the relationship between "grown up" and absorption of information, is probably inversely proportional i.e., **more the age of a person, lesser is his interest in anything happening around him, which is outside his usual circle**. I leave you with his thought, think about it.

<u>Educational Growth</u>

Every person, fortunate enough, gets his chance to acquire educational qualifications. Please mind the word "educational Right from his Kindergarten classes, when he is promoted to his next class it is **assumed** that he has achieved the required proficiency the subjects he was taught. Project this logic, till he graduates in any discipline. It is assumed that he has achieved proficiency in the given subjects. And when acquires post-graduate qualifications he is supposed to have "Mastered" the subject.

The above is in ideal situation. What about practical life? Do you really feel so, when you interact with persons having B.A., B.Sc., B.E., L.L.B. or M.A., MTech, L.L.M., M.Sc. degrees? Do you really feel that they have knowledge contents, justifying their degrees? If, yes is what you feel, I would love to interact with such people, as they are part of a very exclusive club. If your feeling is negative, that is, you feel that degrees have lost their relevance you may be right, in the present scenario in our beloved country. Why such cheapening of education?

Let us analyze!

<u>Qualifications Questioned:</u>

In one of the better advertisements one young man asks the vote demanding leader (neta) about his qualifications, the neta is distinctly uncomfortable. I hope that this may augur the much-wanted effort that our country badly needs. It also set the ball rolling in my mind field about the real relevance of this dreadful thing called as qualification.

If *an Indian* does not know that there is very little relationship between the qualification and the expected response from the qualified person, very few in the rest of the world would know. There is an aspect about the education which in our great country is always questionable and yet very few dares to raise the relevant questions. The relationship between the literacy, education, learning and the subsequent application of the learning is very rarely explained by the factories of qualifications, rampant in our country. The qualifications without verification of the content of what the student may have or not in most cases is the root cause of almost all current problems in our country. We donate qualifications not because the students deserve but because they need them. The degree of differentiation is there but over all picture remains grimly discolored.

Take an example of matriculation. I feel that there is may be 10 different ways (make one or two more or less) in which people get their first public qualification. What is the equivalence? No body knows. If somebody knows he does nothing about it. The SSC, HSSC, ICSE, CBSE are ingredients of confusion which is carried out till the last. The person with 33% and person with 95% get the same qualification. Further there is neither a confirmed method to verify the veracity of the presented qualification nor the methods by which the percentage is obtained. There is a big contribution of the internal marks, favoritism and shameless flaunting of certain students over the rest, which creates the basic disbelief in the system. Unfortunately, even after so many acknowledged academics working together (at least outwardly) have not been able to find any worthy replacement, though various impulsive experiments have been carried out at cost of the poor students, nothing worthwhile has been achieved. The reason is that we are probably finding reasons from a wrong set. It is said that one can not find solutions to illogical problems by logical ways. If you have any doubts, you are most welcome to check the marks of any ward of any head of the institution. The glitter is there for a while and starts withering away as soon as the first stretching is round the corner. The further qualifications are no different and the results are for all of us to see and check. The engineers, doctors, architects and other categorized professionals have legal degrees and no body can question them as far as that aspect is concerned. There are many compulsions due to which the institutes donate the degrees; after all they are **running business** as any other Indian company. The cause for opening an institution is very rarely the knowledge or any thing else even remotely connected, which is a sad state of affairs. The basic infrastructure, the facilities are atrocious. It is known that most of the new medical colleges may not have even a lab and if they have a lab, they may not have a dead body for the dissection. So, the first body they may see is the gullible patient who may not know what sort of trap he is caught in.

The business fraternity was the first sufferer. They started to have their own selection methods in total disregard for the claimed qualifications by the candidate. The selected candidate is further subjected to a grueling training and he is continued only as and when he successfully completes the training.

How can one compare students from different regions having distinctly different standards of fair and unfair means? There is a huge gap between the learning and the qualification, which is increasing in a geometrical proportion with every passing year. Interaction with the candidates for a small period is enough for the litmus test of his plus or minus qualities. One very serious aspect of the qualifications is whether the student has really undergone the trials and toils or he has simply chosen to pay the greedy teachers for his thesis and other such *inconsequential* details. Most of the professional colleges offer this facility as *a fringe benefit* for the students. Some teachers have a specialized outfit for this activity which I feel is worse than a murder. It kills the ingenuity of a person, but who is bothered?

The effect of a heterogeneous education system is already very visible on the employment fields and if some thing drastic is not done, the entire credibility in the important field of education of our country would be at stake. Whether it is technical education or the simple humanities the students must achieve the required level of excellence or else we are heading for a disaster that too on a slippery slide.

The first reason that springs to my mind is **separation** of **education** from **learning.** You may get a degree, but have your learnt enough to apply the knowledge? The application of knowledge is possible only if you have learnt your lessons well.

Second reason is probably the haphazard way the "input" is handled, at the stage of admissions. Students, in our country are admitted to various courses, not because they **deserve** but because the **'need'**. People who have used their crooked fingers to disturb the education system, by way of reservations, have done an irreparable damage to the whole sanctity of education. No persons, however great he may be, can induce required levels of **intelligence or competence in the mind of even a single person**, whose capacity has been compromised by way of reservations, and quota systems. Even people, who enjoy the momentary success in such a ghastly mishandling of education system, ultimately shall know that they have been duped.

At each stage, right from the junior classes, our politicians have devised a devilish system to crate a crop of "so called educated" persons, whose qualifications and responses to situations **never** match.

Third reason is that the person from such a quota system, probably **never undergoes a struggle** that is **essential** to create a useful person, in the context of a strong nation. He is admitted depending upon a caste system, passes due to quota system, gets employed because of the quota system, even gets promoted ahead of many deserving colleagues and then even when he retires; he cannot come out the "Ghetto" mentality. He, may be, is good, but nobody accepts it. Imagine the extent of tension he must undergo through out his life, when he knows that he does not deserve the qualification, he is donated by some populist measures of some politicians, who do not mind holding the pride and prestige of a country at a stake, just to earn few more rupees.

Reservation, in the any intellectual activity is rubbish with a capital 'R'. Agreed, that some people have suffered at the hands of their fellow countrymen, but, then there are better ways of compensating and augmenting. Financial help, proper training facility, encouragement for the **genuine deserving** people, could have produced much better results. Due to the present arrangement, <u>nobody is happy</u>, as those who are benefited have to live with a **stigma** attached, and those who bear the brunt of reservations, keep demanding natural justice. Ironically, this total movement of 'Dalits' was started to get rid of the stigma, but as things stand today, they have created their own world full of stigmas, prejudices, in-sufficiency and ridicule.

How it hampers the growth on a personal, orgnisational, as well as national level is already experienced by every self-respecting Indian.

Earlier a doctor use to be a doctor. Now,

A doctor is categorised - into

- open category merit only
- open category payment seat
- reserved category

.

Now, I have to *seriously* think before I go to a 'government hospital' or any unknown doctor, for that matter, for getting medical attention.

I would love to know how many politicians, who have medical colleges, get themselves or their family treated at their won institutions. Why they have to go to United States or United Kingdom, for getting treatment even for a bout of cold or flue? Because, they surely know the correct worth of students churned out by their institutions.

Why I have tried to deal with this very delicate topic? It is for a simple reason that the sacred relationship between the proficiency levels, expertise levels with the corresponding degrees is violated. Now and even in future you can never be sure about any qualification doled out by an Indian University. The basic integrity of the education giving institution has been questioned and has been found deficient in more than one aspect.

Coming back to educational growth of human being: Worldwide, a person has to achieve some skill, which is why he educates himself, has to hone these skills, so he gets work experience, and apply these skills, so as to generate resources for himself, his family and his beloved nation.

<u>Social Growth</u>:

We love to talk about the society. Social growth comprises of three basic parts relating to –

- a family
- society
- an image

Humans as well as animals are necessarily a part of an establishment which, when operates in a way it should, offers a comfortable and acceptable "give and take" way of life. The institution of work as well as division of labor, are terms which have been used all along, by the social scientists, from times immemorable. Unless, there is effective (social) interaction between the constituents these words have no significance. Very much alike to a mere screw or a nut in a big sophisticated machine. By itself and in isolation, the screw has no meaning, but when fitted at a right place, it helps the sophisticated machine to run productively. This is one reason for which a man should never say "What can I do single handedly?" I f he knows his place and powers; he alone can change a lot and that too, for his own, as well as for his family and for his nation. When an individual talks about his inability to change anything for a worthwhile existence, he must remember that would have been and shall be changed by only those people who are branded as **"unreasonable".** He should also remind himself constantly that his present would, his present (taken for granted) comforts, his day to day "automatic" functioning are certainly due to same unreasonable, inadjustible attitude and belief level of some person in the past. If you still have some hesitation in accepting this, please take a look at the following list:

- Airplane - Internet
- Helicopter - Telephones / Fax
- Railways - TV
- Concorde - Bulbs / Tube Lights
- X-Rays - Xerox
- Antibiotics - Plastics
- Lasers - Vitamins

Given above are the names of some products. My question to you is "Can you find anything common?" Please try.

The point is simple. All these things were considered **impossible** before they were invented.

And, if we are fortunate enough, to enjoy the comforts and convenience offered by these wonderful products, we owe it to the "hard nuts" that had implicit faith in their projects. Today if we are better housed, better educated, better fed, than any other time in the entire history of a mankind, we should show our gratitude to all the great inventors and discovers who had courage to swim against the current, and reach their goal.

The growth of a society starts from growth of an individual or self, a family of this 'self', and subsequently ends up in a community or the nation.

The individual is a prototype of the society. What he thinks as an individual and propagates the thought process to his progeny or his social circle, decides the fate of the society. If the individual is educated, happy, conscious of his duties, sincere, it shall ultimately result in the overall effectiveness of the society and its functioning.

In India, we are still functional or alive as a society, is mainly due to the intrinsic value and judgment of a common Indian. I am sure if the "leaders" were to govern this wonderful society, we would have been a case, very much like Mohenjo Daro and Harrappa civilizations, which have perished.

Every Indian today knows the worth and value of these so-called leaders, he knows the destructive capacity of leaders at municipal corporation level, at a district level, at a state level and finally at the level of the parliament. One wonders whether the "leaders" who **behave** or most of the times **do not behave** in a way they should, can really do anything worthwhile for the betterment of the society. The average Indian knows the usual discount factors, how to apply them, when they listen to these "leaders". Whenever the "leader" starts speaking about 'service' (seva), almost all Indians, irrespective of their education, social status and communication skills, have a wry and bitter smile on their face.

This smile is a **true certificate** of all the **'seva'** (supposedly, self-less service to the people) the "leaders" have forcibly offered to the average Indians. All the foreign invaders, foreign rulers could not have damaged India, as these so called "leaders" have damaged in last 60 years.

In such a scenario, the individual Indian has an immense responsibility on his shoulders. He should bear in mind that if his beloved country has to survive the rapacious attitude of (not the outsiders) the "leaders" he has to be strong and judicious. He has to raise his level of thinking beyond himself, his community and then only he can hope to make his country, *Sujalam, Suphalam* (plenty of water, plenty of fruits). The average Indian should always remember that if he discharges his duty in a way he should, his country shall eventually prosper.

When an individual is born, he is a part of family. When he ties his nuptial knot, he adds one more family to the society. All such families create a society, which is a characteristic of a nation.

The actual state of a nation and what others perceive it, to be, can be a very interesting case study. Yes, I am talking about **'image'** of the country.

Whatever an individual does or does not have a tremendous bearing on the creation of an image of India.

What a custom officer does at the airport, what a cabdriver does at the outside the airport, has an immense impact, on the creation of the **image.** The Indian should understand that the extra money – may be a hundred or a thousand, he is demanding from a foreigner **becomes the price of an Indian Image. Your country's pride is sold at that one hundred extra. Is India so cheap? Think about it.**

Here, I would like to tell you two stories, once concerning a Japanese person and the other of a lowly placed reception clerk in a hotel in USA.

1. One of my friends went to Japan for reading his study paper at a conference. Subsequent to the conclusion of the conference, he wanted to shop for certain items. He went out of his hotel, and like we do in our country, he tried to find out as to where he could get the best and smart deal. He asked his escort about this. My friend was shocked by the answer the got from his escort. "Any where! Sir! In all places you will get quality goods at a reasonable price. Because in Japan everything we manufacture is of top-class quality and at affordable price". Said his escort.

How about our own beloved country? Can you imagine this happening in India? We have families who specialize in liaison and promise the best deals.

2. The second story is about a reception clerk in a hotel at New York. The young lady was looking forward to go to her home on a cold, frosty night. Her shift was to end in about fifteen minutes.

A customer walked into the foyer of the hotel, somehow due to usual overbooking or some such mistake, the hotel was full. The lady knew that she was in a spot. She came out with a dazzling smile, offered a towel and a steaming cup of coffee. By the time when the customer was warm and slightly better off, she told him that she had taken liberty to book him, in an adjacent hotel, which even though was not as good as her own, but was up to the mark. She had already moved the luggage in a cab and then very politely asked the person to move to the hotel. The parting statement was a sorry, a hop and promise of better service next time.

By then the lady was well beyond her normal duty and duty hours. She did not know that her little initiative could help the hotel to a great extent. The customer in the story was a big shot in a leading car manufacturing company and in spite of the discomfort; he was so impressed with the attitude of the inconsequential lady at the reception desk that he recommended to his organization to make it obligatory for his company persons to stay in the same hotel, whenever required. The lady did not know that the marketing staff of her hotel was desperately trying to lure this account for the last so many years.

Is the point clear?

The Japanese escort or this little lady at the reception did some thing to help the image building of his country and her organization.

Are we really growing up to all these aspects? How do we place ourselves, in front of our country or the country comes first? Think about it.

<u>Organizational Growth</u>

Whenever we utter this word, an organisation, what do we see? Do we see a group of people, engaged in an activity, achieving some pre-decided common goal? If yes, then the organisation is where it should be.

An organisation in most cases is a manifestation of single individual's dream. Someone, who is later claimed as a visionary, had seen something, and believed in something, worked very hard to create, results in an organisation. Till the time the person can cope up with his vision and deliver, everything keeps on growing. But subsequently, due to various reasons, such as expansion, diversification, the organisation starts getting decentralized. And it is here the problems start. By this time, the original creative individual has been put on the wall in form of a photograph with a 'Chandanhaar'*, below the photograph is a caption "our Inspiration". Onwards this stage, the organisation starts suffering from inflated egos, erratic decisions etc.

Why this happens? Does it mean that the people who subsequently control the organisation are not as good as the founder himself? Outwardly and apparently not! The juniors, in most cases are better educated, better qualified, but then why they can not do what the old man did? The season is simple. The old man "owned" his dream. He worked for his dream. He took his own risks and weighed his own stakes. It is also seen that generally the third generation onwards the things start to once again fall in proper place.

The growth of an organisation is very complex issue. Classically it has been still debated whether commitment or professionalism is vital for the correct growth of an organisation. I feel that each of the above factors in isolation has no power, but can be of immense value, if a concept of a "committed professionalism" is promoted. The commitment of a professional should be time bound, result oriented and duplicable. Then only the organisation can grow. The knowledge about generalities and specifics can be imparted by intensive trainings, proper induction schedules.

The growth of an organisation is directly proportional to the **vision** of the Chief Executive. Where the CE **sets his eyes** upon, can eventually make or break an organisation.

- Can he **project** himself at least 10 years in the future?
- Does he have a **contingencyplan?**
- Does he really understand global economics?
- Does he **compromise** on quality of his production?
- Is he **aware** about the "perception of people" about his company?
- How **often** he diversifies?
- What are his **responses** to anything new?
- Is he **sure** of his organisation's capacity to sustain the present-day levels?

Whether the organisation grows or stops to grow can be because of some sensible answers to the above questions.

The second part in growth of an organisation is the development.

While the organisation is maintaining the present-day levels, day the day and year to year activities, is there someone who is thinking about its future? The development is growing towards a pre-planned goal. In a very dynamic scenario of trade today, where a technology by itself can be obsolete in a short span of time and hence discarded, this aspect of development can be of vital importance.

Development is generally discussed **for the absence of** it, in most cases, at a very painful post-mortem. Why development is needed? One line answer to this **"He who stop being better, stops being goods".** Development is a constant urge to be better and hence should be ever present phenomenon.

<u>**Spiritual Growth**</u>

Generally, people associate spirituality with something they are supposed to do when they retire, from active life. Further, it is also confused with "pooja path" (worshipping) and or the processes that are laid down by religious preachers. I feel spirituality is extremely personal and it does concern me and my Almighty, as I see Him or understand Him. Spiritual growth to me is how close I am to my supreme spirit, God.

Ideologically, in Indian philosophy the life of man is divided in to four *ashramas* (phases of life), such as *Brahmacharya, Gruhasthashrama, Vanprasthashram and Sanyasashram.* In each to these phases a normal human being is supposed to do certain duties towards himself and his society. But it certainly does not mean that these phases cannot overlap. If a human being does, what is supposed to be done by him, he may achieve nirvana or ultimate peace.

A story comes to my mind regarding the life period of human beings. It is said that when God created the earth animals, he gave each species a life of 40 years. However, man was not satisfied and hence requested the Creator to give some additional years. Interestingly though, some animals were sue that they had more then enough life. On a mutual understanding the God gifted humans 20 years each of donkey, monkey and owl. To what effect we all now know! In a life of approximately 100 years man leads parts of his life very similar to the lives of original donors. What we have to realise is that being the smartest animal we have that much more responsibility.

Spiritual growth is very important in a life of human being as it alone gives a correct posture and sense of balance.

The basis of spirituality is to know the secrets of the birth and death. Nachiketa, in the kathopnishad, went all out to find the meaning of death. Yamraj, the in-charge deity for death related function told him that nobody can answer to "Nachiket's" questions. It is very difficult to explain the functioning of the universe and hence humans in all religions have talked about God.

An atheist (who does not believe in God) shall say that God is the imagination of some people. Maybe it is! (One of the most relevant question that must be asked is why only humans need a god, no other animal needs such a complex manifestation to lead a successful life.) But, what a wonderful way to create a fear, respect and regulation in the minds of otherwise unruly, and selfish humans to keep them generally on the right track?

Today, humans have been able to produce the DNA – the life particle, in the laboratory condition. But even today we do not know much about how a string of chemicals, whether helical or not, actually produces life. We know how to replicate DNA or RNA, but still need, a primer for the replication. We have not been able to create or synthesize the molecule itself.

Secondly, humans with all present technical resources have not been able to unravel the mystery of death. What happens in that small fraction of time, which leaves a permanent impact on the body, is yet not at all known. The in vivo to in vitro transformation still proves to be a big journey.

I feel the day man understands "the creation of life"' along with "the end of life", the whole concept of spirituality shall undergo a sea of change. Let us hope that the new knowledge shall lead to further progress.

The worst quoted and cited sentence from Geeta is "No one gets anything before the scheduled time and given destiny) People do not do anything as a result. Lord Krishna never meant anything of the above. He never said anything about not doing your karma. The essence of what He said is **"You do your karma and do not worry about results; I shall be responsible for results."**

Spiritualism is finding a way to lead our own life in a way which should be effective and productive. It does not mean running away from life, nor does it mean to be ritualistic. All great leaders have condemned renunciation because of failure in your worldly duties. You should not urn away from life, because you cannot correctly lead it. Such deserters cannot find the real meaning of life, forge the God.

These days some television channels have some time slots reserved for spiritual discourses, where as, some channels are exclusively dealing with spirituality. Please understand that this actually is more **marketing oriented** rather that **God oriented.** Spiritual achievements can never be easy and unless you are ready to put in the necessary efforts (Sadhana) you can never have the spiritual enlightenment. Spiritual enlightenment has very little to do with '*Chamatkar*' or a miracle. On the other hand, Siddhi (the chamatkar phase) is a major hurdle, which the **sadhak** (one who does sadhana) has to cross, to be anywhere near, the final enlightenment.

Spiritualism is a complex subject and unless one reaches a certain level of understanding and comprehension, one should not attempt to venture. Secondly, unless you have someone as Guru, it is said that you should not attempt to solve the riddles. The multi-dimensional aspects and theories are as complex as any in theoretical physics. However, you try, can you imagine your world in 4 dimensions? Something, similar is spiritualism. One, who understands the ultimate truth, is also aware about the value and hence does not easily part with it to someone not worthy enough.

Whether Mother Teresa performed any miracle or not, is not he matter one should discuss. Whether she had a vested interest or she was really serving the human race in their worst conditions is immaterial. **The whole life of the great lady is itself a miracle**. What she gave to the poor and oppressed people in Kolkata, is beyond any testing. Whether you call her a saint or not, does not in any way reduce the great job, she did in the service of the most neglected section of human society.

Conversely, there are so many saints, fakirs, babas who claim that they are gods in themselves. I do not know what to say? You have your own scale to accept or reject their claim. The major / minor miracles they are doing are not worth a penny as far as the reduction in sufferings of human beings is concerned.

Spirituality to me is to lead a life with a set of moral values, committing as few mistakes as possible, setting up and following your own ethical and moral standards, doing your worldly duties as perfectly as possible, doing your social and national duties. The journey fro Purusha to Purushottam (human to super human) follows the routine path of normal life.

Spirituality to me is to accept a fact after it has passed the test of time, and has been any proved. What is spiritual about accepting that earth revolves round the sun after hundreds of years? Proximity to the ultimate truth, if there is such a thing existing, is spirituality. Answers to the reason of our existence, the control of the same can be the first step to understand the divinity and spirituality.

Spiritualism should never be confused with fanaticism. A fanatic can never be close to God. History has shown that fanatics have always been a trouble for human beings. Fanatics are very extremely positioned, about something which in itself may not be permanent. All "sins" for which fanatics gave their lives, and have destroyed the lives of thousands of fellow humans, are now "Gone". Neither do they exist nor their "isms"!

In a country where it has been taught that one can pray with a petal, a leaf, water and other such non costly, easily available items, it pains me to see the fanfare of *puja*, or a mass or an "*urs*".

What you think about your God is strictly and absolutely personal. The moment you want to **show off your worshipping, you go away from God**. In fact, the more the rituals, the more is the possibility of the activity which as nothing to do with God. The temples, mosques, the majors, the churches, the gurudwaras and all such places are and **should be places of utmost reverence, cleanliness and holiness**. If you cannot maintain this simple logic, I do not think you have anything to do with God. Ever increasing commercialization of religion may ultimately end in destruction of the religion and its followers.

Consider this, a doctor who does not attend a patient, because he is busy in worshipping, can he ever achieve spiritual peace? A judge, accepting a bribe and giving a wrong judgment, subsequently going to Kashi or to a church, can he ever achieve peace? And person who does not do his duties and talks about spiritual achievement is a big humbug and should be dealt with scant respect.

Religion whenever has been bent by people, whether the king (raja) or subjects (praja), has always created problems, and has ruined so many lives, cities and even civilizations.

Spiritual growth has a part which most of us are supposed to know. This generally deals with what we show to the people around us. We like to think that people should know us as pious, holy, God fearing and with a strong moral base. To crate this impression what do we do? The impression once created needs a constant reassurance to ourselves mainly. To keep it up, we are seen at temples, churches, mosques, gurudwaras and all such places of worship. We show off by doing so many things. If you don't believe this just visit any temple or a church. You shall see a sample of humanity doing so many funny looking things.

Spirituality is an inside phenomenon. Like they say character is tested in darkness, meaning, what you do when nobody in watching you is what you are in reality. The moment, you want that people should consider you as holy and pious person because of you outside gestures, you be sure that you have missed the entire point, of being spiritual. Whatever you do, you should be always and permanently be aware that you cannot hide from the omnipotent God. He certainly knows and probably keeps a track of what you are, what you do, and most importantly what you deserve.

Spiritual growth comes not from the rituals, but from the basic knowledge, that you are doing what you are supposed to do, your duties towards yourself, family, nation. If you know that you are correct, then automatically, you are surer and more confident that the God is nearer you. So many stories have been narrated about how a person missed a lifetime's opportunity to see and interact with God. Meaning thereby whatever you do in a quest to find the God, to ensure the blessings of the God, you should do same things for the most common, inconsequential person around you, because you never know in what from God has decided to bless you.

So, spirituality should not be limited to your presence in temple or church or a mosque, but it should ideally be a daylong process. Meditation mood should persist through out your daily routine. If you can maintain a holy, pious attitude, all through your day and daily routine, I think you may turn out to be the most spiritual person. The interaction of your good deeds and your daily routine can alone give you the most sought-after inner peace.

We have tried to understand some basic forms of growth and we would be dealing the other aspects of growth in the next parts of this discussion.

***

CHAPTER THREE

What Makes Anything Grow?

<u>What Makes Anything Grow?</u>

Before we embark upon the factors resulting in growth you should ask me a logical question which is "Why should anything grow?" Why we need to grow? More importantly why we need to grow on a continued basis?

Growth is phenomenon which relates with size, volume, content, ability, against one very significant parameter, which is time. Growth in isolation has no meaning, or it can be also said that if growth is to be converted into a cashable resource, it has to be in relation with time. Such growth can be called as progress.

What grows naturally is generally less worthy in terms of economic worth. A mango tree bearing fruits is important but a mango orchard, grown and cared for, in a deliberate fashion is far more productive. The process of improved agriculture has changed the entire food scenario in out beloved country. I remember, (Milo) the red and stinking jowar or /PL480 (Wheat) and its roti in 1964. The younger generation in the present day of pizza, burgers, cannot probably imagine how horrible the taste was. It further became worse with the knowledge that the horrible tasting 'food supply' was given to us, the poor Indians, as 'alms. To cap it all it was published that the grains which were supplied to us, the poor Indians were considered unworthy even for the 'cattle' in that particular country. On this background the food situation today should be weighed. The pride of "self-sufficiency" can be felt in a correct way, subsequent to the tasting of Milo/PL 480. Today, every time I eat a full meal fit for humans – I thank gratefully to Shri Lal Bahadur Shastri, Dr. M.S. Swaminathan, the great agriculturist, Dr. Kurian, the father of the white revolution (Amul), and so many other persons, who with practically no worthwhile resources, 'grew' to "legends" and in the process made their country – a proud and self-sufficient nation.

The story should in some way throw light on need to grow. We need grow to become self-sufficient, for our self-esteem, to achieve our aspirations and goals.

Further we have to understand though growth is associated with vitality; any rewarding growth does not come automatically. As human beings, we know that the birth and death are the "decided" events. So, when we grow, we should bear in mind that in a way it is a march towards the 'end'. Yet we know that during this limited time (we do not know if we will see the tomorrow) we have to grow, achieve all things we want and most importantly leave something behind for our descendents. Classically it has been said that one should check whether he has done anything worthwhile, to ensure betterment over the state of the world he had inherited.

The most important reason to grow is to avoid 'stagnation'. Continuous growth alone can save you from becoming stagnated or stale. The will to grow, the will to better our present day lots is like recharging our batteries. Any amount of skill, if left unused is surely a waste, is the long run.

What makes anything grow?

Once we know the need to grow, we should subsequently try to find out the reasons for growth. The first and foremost is a genuine will to grow. Unless there is a need felt from inside, very rarely growth is achieved.

Growth is due to life cycle of a plant or an animal. This growth is "automatic" to say so, as it is governed by nature. The seed is sown, it germinates, grows into a plant, a shrub or a tree, it flowers, it gets its flowers pollinated, it reproduces fruits and lastly gets it s seeds dispersed, to begin a new journey towards further evolution.

The plants have undergone the life cycle again and again, over the ages. Besides what they do for the world is of immense value and vital importance. They give greenery to the world, they release oxygen in the atmosphere, create rain pockets; give the animals a steady source of food, fruits, vitamins and medicines, at practically no cost. **It is only when man intervenes the problems start.** One of my professors always said that the plants are more **evolved than animals,** as they are capable of producing whatever they need, in a sedentary state. Think about it.

The patents for Neem, Tulsi, charcoal in a tooth paste as well as, Basmati rice is a big irony. What is the intelligent contribution of the person in the development of these freely and naturally available resources? Why should he reap the benefits from an otherwise freely available plant? The benefits of such plants like the ones given above, along with turmeric, black pepper, clove, mint and so many others were available and should be available for generations to come. But some extra smart people and countries cannot see the light. I can understand patents for inventions like bulbs, stereos, TVs, because they were creation of some particular person's enterprise and intellectual involvement. If natural resources are subject to patents, royalties the future scenario can be utterly horrible. Just imagine in the future after about 100 years, some god forsaken evil mind, manages to patent air, the sunlight, the wind, the rainfall, rate of heart beat and the so- called intelligent society accepts to pay royalty on the creations by the nature.

i. Standard air intake by each human hung during respiration. May be a standard volume say 1.5 liters air / per intake of inhalation. Anybody exceeding this volume has to pay, say 10 paise, per breathing cycle. Can you imagine the damage?

ii. For every extra mm of rainfall, the respective country ha to pay royalty.

iii. You heart is supposed to beat 72 times per minute; if it exceeds you pay royalty on each extra heartbeat.

Sounds Horrible! Is it?

But remember that 100 years ago, patenting neem, Tulsi, turmeric, also would have sounded horrible. **Man has always been his own greatest enemy**. To this effect an Urdu couplet which says:

"Where is the need of any enemy?

When we have friends like you?"

The second factor, responsible for growth is the restlessness of an individual. He conceives something however impossible in the present context – and then follows up his project. He is restless till he achieves what he had conceived. The people are the ones, who are responsible for so many areas of growth inhuman society.

The curiosity, the quest for knowledge is probably the single largest factor for growth. Classically it is said, that the apples always fall down and they have done for ages. But it took a curious mind of Newton to subsequently formulate the theory of gravity.

Thirdly, continuous action forms a major factor in resulting growth. This concept when modified resulted in "Economy of Scale". It has been exploited all over the world for achieving growth. The continuous action creates a near perfect model which ensures the smooth functioning, by way of continuous evaluation and improvement.

Competition is one more reason for the growth. The constant fear of competition in any segment creates a terrific growth pattern. Ask any industrialist and he is always thinking about expansion, by way of increasing the installed capacity or readymade capacity available by way of takeovers. Companies like Ponds, Lipton, Brooke-Bond, now are a part of a conglomerate which is a sign enough to know the nature of business in the next decade or two.

To succeed in the fierce competition one has to renovate, redesign, all his available products and resources which really changes the scene. The technology is the single most important factor for the growth and the changing technology keeps everyone on his toes. One cannot relax for a bit of time or else he is relegated to background or even to extinction. Can you see my point? So many products have gone away; so many technologies have gone away. The constant surge towards betterment is a factor, which is supposed to create growth.

Advertisement and promotions are the monsters of the last century. The extra ordinary pressure created by advertisement, on the psyche of gullible customers is to be seen to be believed. I shall try to give one example.

Problem – Dandruff in the hair. And in last 10-15 years all cosmetics manufacturers have concentrated on anti- dandruff shampoos and conditioners. Medically, dandruff is a minor skin ailment and no man has been reported dead due to dandruff, in the entire history of mankind.

But the impression the advertisements create, in the vulnerable minds of younger generation is quite anomalous to say the least. The way the star reacts when he sees the white particles on a black blazer, is so exaggerated he might have seen a leper, or a rabid dog. Overselling without any responsibility and accountability is a major bane of almost all Indian as well as international advertisements. Limited exposure, no awareness of the ground reality, creates such haphazard advertisements. I feel the products are promoted with a blatant disregard towards truth. **Henceforth, whenever you see an advertisement, I implore you to think about reality. <u>Also, imagine life without these products</u> and you will be surprised to know that, to lead a healthy life you may not need any of such products.**

The relationship between a product promoted and the theme can be probably measured by a calipers scale. A shaving cream is always promoted by an unclad lady and a toilet cleaning agent is promoted by a man. The vulgarity, projected in advertisement is to be seen to be believed. I many remember ad, the recall is achieved, but I may never buy the product.

But in spite of all rubbish, advertisements still contribute in the growth of a product, arguably for a shorter span of time.

Growth is also a result of unnatural circumstances. It has been seen that mankind has always progressed in leaps and bounds, during the times of adversities. The situations, unimaginable, during normal time have helped mankind to grow. Like the masks sales increase during the recent corona outbreak in Pune, and other parts of India. I do not justify any of such means, but the fact remains, the growth was achieved.

I shall cite one example. It has been reported that during the World War II, German Doctors experimented on Jews using them as biological samples. What is the pressure at which human artery bursts, what is the maximum temperature human skin can endure? What happens if females are impregnated with animal sperms, how a human heart reacts to various stimuli, such as shocks, poisons. All such experiments have contributed to knowledge of human biology and medical applications.

Once again, I condemn the means, as all decent human beings must, but the fact remains that the growth was achieved.

Adversity also ignites the latent capacity of human beings. A frail and delicate lady is reported to have lifted her car to save her child.

In the times of Chhatrapati Shivaji Maharaj, a woman climbed down the most difficult cliff, in total darkness as she desperately wanted to feed her child. How does this happen? If you want to know the "impossible" nature, you are welcome to see Raigarh Fort, in Maharashtra, during the broad daylight and you will realise, what I am talking about.

Apart from a host of positive factors, negative factors also contribute to growth of a person. Jealousy is one such feeling that has contributed to growth of so many persons. Jealousy about other person, who we feel is more accomplished and successful than us, constantly reminds us about our destination. Till we reach there we do not intend to stop. The fire of jealousy burns brightly and it does not allow us to rest. But personally, I feel that positive factors which induce growth are a better condition. Jealousy oriented or any other negative factor-oriented growth is generally very painful, less satisfactory and results, even if successful, cannot be usually enjoyed. The fierce competition with the person is only one sided and as the same may not be even noticed by the person, we are jealous of. More importantly, by the time we reach pre-decided level of accomplishment, the original person has achieved many times more than the current bench mark.

Their enjoyment, which otherwise would have been a near complete feeling is not there; because a fresh booster dose of jealously is ready, due to the fresh achievements of the person, which started the wild goose chase.

Growth is also in many cases due to revenge mentality. One may grow, achieve the impossible when he pursues revenge, but can never be happy. Wither in the course of action or when it is over. So pre-occupied is the person with his revenge that he does not realise the wastage of his time, talent which he could have otherwise utilized in a much better way. Again, when the revenge is taken, he confronts a vacuum and usually he perishes rather than prosper.

***

CHAPTER FOUR

Have You Planned Your Growth?

<u>Have You Planned Your Growth?</u>

Why should any one plan anything? Why should anyone strive to fulfill his aspirations? Why should any one stretch beyond his normal capacity a achieve something he wants?

If anyone does not do anything, what happens? Nothing. Nothing really happens. A man is born, lives like an "animal", and then dies. Is it really how it should be?

It is told in Hindu Philosophy, that a human is born after he goes through a tedious journey of 8400000 (8.4 million) species. Subsequent to this arduous travel through the unknown, he gets his life as a human. Do you now realise the worth of a single human life? Whether you believe this logic or not, one thing is sure that human life is precious. Now that you have got it, what do you do about it? You can do something, achieve, deliver or you just walk out of the scene as empty handed as they do. An interesting observation, about an infant when he / she is born and a person when dies, ha always fascinated me. A child when born has his fists tightly closed as if in a resolve, but when the person dies his palms are open – as if to show that he has achieved nothing. Even Alexander, the Great, had same feeling about his achievements.

With all this knowledge it becomes of paramount importance that we need to plan out growth. As already said in this book, two events the birth and the death are the only certainties as soon as one is born, his death is a decided event. Though we know that we are death bound, how often we plan our death? It is something as weird as thinking about a divorce, while taking marriage vows. We do not do it; we do not want even to think about it.

A very interesting experiment was done in one of the premier institutes of business management. The students, who were passing out of a management course, were asked about their future plans, and the relevant data was maintained. Some students said they will do this and that, while others (very few about 2 to 3 %) had exact and written down goals. 20 years later a follow up survey was undertaken. In spite of a very highly valued degree, only 2 to 3% students were having what they had wanted – 2 to 3% who <u>knew what they wanted</u>. The rest were actually doing this or that.

This experiment very elaborately explains the value of written down goals. If you happen to be a person who has a written down goal – nothing is said about actual achievements – you are welcome to the "2 to 3% club", on the global scene. Very exclusive, isn't it?

It has been said that if you want to grow, begin with the end in mind. The picture of a "successful you" as you perceive, should be the starting point of your growth. The tricky and often inaction causing question of "why and what", is already answered when you have a written down goal. What remains is "when". The inactivity is caused by the word 'if'. If I do not achieve what I want, or if I fail, are the questions which must have paralyzed millions of creative people. The world is a big loser, as the world will probably never know about the extent of how many wonderful things were conceived, but never achieved, because of this question.

Classically it has been said "Whatever the mind of man can conceive and believe, it can achieve (Napoleon Hill -in the book - Think & Grow Rich).

The problem in the minds of we, common men, starts because we limit even our imagination. Under the garb of rationalism, reality, probability, capacity, history, experience of our elders, we try to play very safe, as far as when we decide what we want to be. The fear of the individual further cuts down the size of his future and his growth.

We may save ourselves from ridicule by playing safe, but we in true sense we ruin our entire life. We lose the very purpose f our life.

Never limit your imagination. It does not cost you a penny, whether you conceive to be billionaire or a pauper. Our forefathers tell us that whatever we utter in our house in automatically granted by the Vastudevta. The Goddess says "Tathastu", (meaning a blessing from Goddess of house, "You shall get what you want").

Let us now discuss an over-exposed word 'Dream'. The word which was mostly used in cases of poets and other conventionally accepted people, as impractical, now has been used, and over exposed by the new culture of networking organisations. But, do we really need to be cynical or sarcastically about this genuinely interesting word? As I have always said **"What you do today is your present what you may have done is your past, but the only way you can live in your future is through your dreams".** Dreams are powerful and may be, they are the single, foremost reason, for whatever inventions and discoveries mankind has achieved. The extent of **virtual reality** achieved through dreams is very colorful and full of positive impacts. Books have been written on dreams, about not allowing any person to steal you dreams. You get human form of life once only, that too after a long journey through mazes of evolutionary process and because of this sole reason, you should make the most of this wonderful opportunity. The basic fact that you are born **as a human** should tell you that you are **very special and exclusive**. Think about this. Dreams can be a powerful means to impart 'meaning' to you otherwise drab and monotonous life.

So, if you feel self-conscious while you plan your growth, please be strong enough to bury your self-consciousness and learn to see things in a way you want, learn to change the ways, so that you can achieve whatever you want, by putting in all the efforts needed, and succeed.

Once you decide what you want, the first thing you should do is to put it on a paper. This is the first deliberate act you should undertake, to ensure that you do no miss the idea. Second equally important step is to put a date by which you would like to accomplish the same. Your dream along with a self accepted date is a very powerful combination, culminating in the "setting of goal". The moment you do this you are a different person.

The procedure involved hereafter is very important. If you do right things at a **right time**, along with **right tools**, in the company of **right people**, with a **right attitude**, you shall be **right where** you wish to be.

***

CHAPTER FIVE

Action Plan for Growth

<u>Action Plan for Growth.</u>

This is an aspect which I wish to deal on three levels. The first level is the personal level, to be followed by organizational level and finally the national level. People ask me why not global? And I answer that if all nations are engaged, in what they should be, without meddling with other nation's activity, stop playing big brother, forget iron curtains, get away from domination and intention to suppress and oppress, the global circumstances shall be automatically set right. Moreover, I am more concerned about myself, my family, my society and my nation, which I feel deserve a great deal more that what they have. We as a country, have never attacked any other country, never been barbaric as compared to out invaders. We have always given willingly and some times under coercion and history bears out the fact that we always have maintained a better posture. All invaders attacked our country, because they did not have the right balance of mental and material resources. So, without bothering for the looters and pirates of the remaining world, let us first clean the present mess which is a creation of our own people and the ones whom we never wanted to land on the soil of our country. We as Indians have a great and probably ultimate responsibility, to educate the world outside our country.

<u>Plan for Personal Level</u>

As a person, it becomes very personal to what one wants. How badly he wants? Does he think that given a chance; he deserves what he thinks he aspires for? The level, the magnitude of aspirations varies on big pendulum like scale. But in the end, it does not matter, if one achieves what he wants. For a person, who knows what he wants, it becomes slightly easier to chalk out the plan and strategy. Before he really begins the pursuit, he should remember following important things.

1. **That shortage of money should not stop him.**

All big enterprises, all personal feats have been in most cases achieved with no money to begin with. A few rupees have been the starting points for so many of today's glorious and glamorous successes.

2.That life is not fair!

Things are never going to be in the ideal or even favourable conditions. To expect favors or concessions is a result of a low self esteem. In fact, if you know in advance, that you are in for a great fight or tussle, you are better placed. So never search for ideal time, ideal day, ideal place, because it does not happen. **What you have today does matter, you must be able to use it.**

3. **That people are ready to pull you down**

This attitude is a global pastime of many of the fellow humans. If somebody is planning to do something, the first response he receives from his close associates is generally of pure ridicule. They shall tell you with a wicked smile "You cannot do it because no one else has ever done it". The same has been told to each and every inventor, discover, writer, poet, actor, all through the centuries. Just ignore this.

4. **People shall oppose at every step.**

Every move to oppose you should make you more resolute and more serious. Each such move should ignite your inner strength, to make you successful.

*(5) As Shiv Khera put it so beautifully "Winners do not do different things. They do things differently". I think we should be grateful to Mr. Khera for his definition of a winner.

*You can win" – Shiv Khera

(6) Belief building measures should be strictly followed.

Belief can be very automatic; you have it or you do not have it. In the initial stages of planning, you may thrust forward by the mere presence of belief. Subsequently this belief has to be sustained. And this is very difficult unless you have some preplanned measures as a measuring scale.

The belief building measures can be identified as

- Correct Posture - Get it
- Correct technique - Learn it

- Correct Procedure - Follow it
- Correct Language - Use it

And all such means which should be constant, in spite of getting good or bad results, on a temporary basis. The setbacks which are a necessary part of any eventual success can be confidently tackled by the knowledge that you are correct in what you are doing.

Once a person has ensured that he is aware about the earlier discussed problems, he should then subsequently learn, about following phases in everyone's life.

A. Phase of learning and unlearning
B. Phase of acquiring special skills
C. Phase of consolidation of your position
D. Phase pf transfer of knowledge and experience

The personal plan of growth should ideally encompass all these phases, which will effectively mean that the entire active life–span a person is covered.

A. **<u>Phase of learning and unlearning</u>**: - The first phase is relatively easy as an individual is goaded, and in some few cases, properly guided by his parents and teachers into the initial stages of this phase. It has been observed that a person generally is somewhere in 9th or 10th standard; by the time he realizes that he is learning some important lessons of life. Also, it has been seen that most people undergo this vital phase of education without any concrete idea or plans. During this period, he does not even think of the likely problems he shall be facing in the not-so-distant future. The feelings of most of the students interviewed at this stage are very weird. Very similar to the belief that if God has brought us to this world, He shall also arrange to feed us. We all know that somehow it does not work that way. Boys and girls at this phase are very reluctant to even peep into their future, where they might have to struggle. So far in their lives, they have always got what they wanted. In fact, they live a life of comfort and ease, as if they are sponsored, by their parents. Very few realise the pains, extra efforts the parents have to put in to somehow maintain the adopted lifestyle. The top 20% (of students) are different, they realise and put in extra efforts and manage to get out the rat race. The bottom 20% anyhow is insignificant in the context of severe competition. But the 60% in between, are oblivious or pretend to be so, of the extreme competition that lies ahead of them. They somehow believe that they shall be the lucky ones, who shall have a readymade job or a profession, leading into a successful next phase of their lives.

Most people in all over the world present a very casual attitude towards this make-or-break phase.

The education pattern prevailing in on country does not help either. The relationship between the acquired qualification and the level of competence supposed to be achieved is very qualification and the level of competence supposed to be achieved is very questionable, to say the least. Most Bas in our country can hardly write the full form of their degree correctly. The casual attitude towards languages whether, English or Hindi or the mother tongue, reflects very badly in the future. The result is that most of the students cannot read or write or speak any language correctly, throughout their remaining lives. Unfortunately, because of the present employment scenario, these people are somehow employed and they create a chaos that nobody has been able to resolve. A teacher from such a crop can only create replicas of himself. An engineer shall always be in doubt and shall never deliver what he is supposed to. I shudder to even think about the medical scene twenty years from today. Due to lopsided nature of our society, such people who are not competent, can also reap money and become socially acceptable, in spite of being absolute hollow at the core. I feel the education should impart intelligence rather than cleverness. A serious student should learn the subject or topic for himself rather that getting 30 to 40% passing marks. Knowledge acquired in a right manner is the only deposit over which he is likely to get any interest, by way of a job or a profession. The indifferent attitude towards actual learning has been a major factor causing unemployment and general anarchy. One should be able to say for himself, whether he is a doctor or an Engineer or a Lawyer, in the true senses of the word, after he has acquired the corresponding relevant degrees, otherwise these degrees are not worth the paper they are printed on.

Simultaneously, along with learning, another important activity goes on, which is unlearning phase. One has to unlearn many things he might have inadvertently picked up. Bad habits we all know are easy to pick up but very difficult to shed off. During this time an individual has to understand that time taken to work neatly or shoddily is generally same. So why not have, for example.

- Good handwriting instead of bad
- Dress properly instead of being casual
- Use good language instead of profanities
- Find an ideal idol instead of some tin pot leader
- Extend yourself fully instead of shortcuts.
- Actually, do things yourself, instead of paying for them.

I was shocked to know that quite a few teachers in engineering colleges provide a readymade project report to the students. I think this is as dreadful as a murder or even more, as it murders the ingenuity of a person.

Unlearning mainly deals with giving up all such habits, which may prove to be major blockades in the path of success.

(B) <u>Phase of acquiring special skill:</u> - When you are employed, you may understand the actual insufficiency of your education, I always believe that the serous education starts, once the person is employed. Within the vast scope of, mechanical engineering, there are many skills to be specially learnt. A good stenographer (Who is very scarce) can distinguish in self-correspondence, report writing, project / report reparations. One should actually aim at acquiring near wizard like status in his area of interest, so much so that the mere **mention of the job** should be enough to **automatically remind people his name.**

To be successful one should keep on adding different skills to his repertoire. This helps in two ways. The first is that you are always in demand and secondly, it avoids monotony.

(C) <u>Phase of consolidation of your position</u>: - During this phase one has to repeatedly perform beyond the expectation of his colleagues, in a way to assure them that the previous achievement is not a mere fluke. When you accomplish again and again, you create a confidence, in the minds of your employers, clients, associates and all others who matter. This generally results in more lucrative jobs, promotions, better contracts, assignments and ultimately a satisfactory prosperous status.

(D) <u>Phase of transfer of knowledge and experience</u>: - I have seen many people achieving excellent results in the first three phases of their lives. Somehow, they are not able to transfer their knowledge, to the worthy ones they come across. Either they are not able or they are not willing to do so.

If you are not able to transfer your knowledge to someone worthy it shall mean that you will keep on ding what your have been. It becomes tiresome, as it becomes monotonous. You stop growing because you are not doing anything new. Remember this

"If you are smart – your work alone

If your group is smart – you earn".

You earn wealth, respect and most importantly you earn the time to do something new.

Ideally you should prepare at least two individuals who can take up your work, before you are promoted. If you are afraid that by doing so you may lose your job, then, you deserve it. Maybe you have reached your level of incompetence.

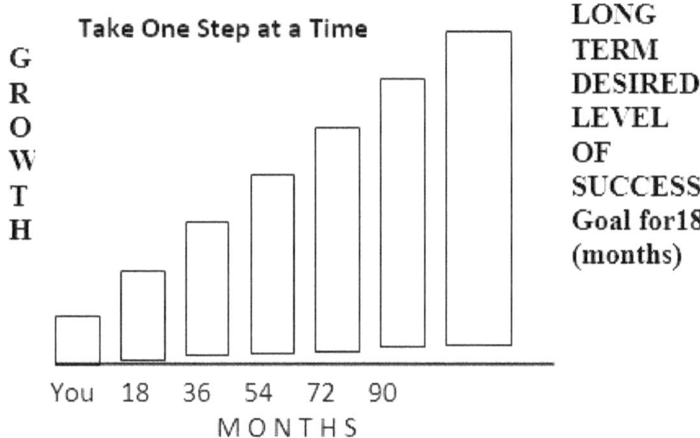

Time-span of 18 Months is important, because it generally covers all seasons, twice.

Action Plan

Action Plan for an Organisation

Organisation is term which encompasses various resources – living as well as non-living – working towards a pre-decided objective. Very few people gave any significant attention, to this now acclaimed, as an important component in the business. In the past it was felt that around an entrepreneur, organisation finds its own way to grow that too without any intentional effort. You may work in, study it, offer consultancy to spy against it, build it or destroy it, in each of the above situation, you have to first <u>understand organisation in a correct way.</u> Is organisation mere group of people? What is the administration function, personal function, finance function, marketing function, legal function and so on and so forth? Does organisation have its own pr-designed path to glory or doom? Can you in each case change the path? This question brings out the most sought after "Leadership function", which affects any organisation by the presence or lack of it.

Why people are given importance in any organisation? May be, because it is the only variable factor! After all, you cannot change the land, machinery, the process, as easily as you can change the people. That people can really effect a change is a myth. The correct sentence should be proper people can really effect a change. And many organisations are working overtime to find a proper mix of people through out their operating life.

If you feel that people in your organisation are not "proper" then check-out. Who brought them in your organisation? Were they proper, before they joined the organisation? What made them go awry after their joining? Or if they were not 'proper', why were they selected, in the first place, to be a part of your organisation? The concept of synergy should be very well understood, as it is so realistically applicable in the case of human interaction, as it is so realistically applicable in the case of human interaction. Humans have an uncanny gift of making, 2+2=5 or 2+2=0. How it is achieved is a separate topic, which needs a special treatise. However, in short synergy is an interesting process where various people while working together, produce much more than the sum total of their respective individual capacities. Suppose three people working together with their positive and negative attributes. In a synergistic situation they produce work for, may be, 6 or 9 people. Positive attributes tend to multiply rather than add, in human interaction. Conversely, the same interaction, between the wrong types, can produce work equivalent to a big zero. Hence it is very important to understand synergy very correctly.

Considering that an ideal organisation has an ideal set of people, what should be ideally the (growth) action plan for such an organisation? The action plan should have a mixed se of objectives, simultaneously, or a single objective to be supported by all other functions.

Classically, the action plan should have following interdisciplinary goals:

1. Product Goals
2. Output Goals
3. System Goals
4. Marketing Goals
5. Social Goals – Society in general

The above are in a random order, and each organisation, can have its own priority depending upon the stage at which it is presently in. Are you in an initiation stage or a consolidation stage or a diversification stage, can decide what sort of priority you may have? And you also remember that you should use simple language, in deciding your goals rather than, the usual jargon dished out.

Any goal you decide should be slightly improbable, but never impossible. It should be a one liner rather than a page long. Something like "100000 in 2024", or "Export to 5 countries in 2025" or any such simple sentence. Preferably it should be decided by the Chief Executive and then he should be able to promote and achieve.

It should prove very interesting to study above five types of goals. It will be varying helpful if you put your inputs in the overall and general picture, which is presented by me. The premise, here is simple that you know your business best.

1) <u>Product Goals</u>:

Most of the organisations are baffled at the question <u>"What business are you in?"</u> The question seems simple, but when an entrepreneur starts to answer it, he finds it difficult. Try to pinpoint. Try to be as specific as you can get.

The products you sell today can be at best, one way to achieve your goals. What you should be able to do preferably is to decide product characteristic goals. You should be able to decide whether or not emphasize on quality, quantity, style, variety, ease to get, distribution, USP (Unique Sales Proposition), novelty, usability or reusability, periodic new product introduction, price as compared to the competition, probable life period of a product, subsequent 'better' product, and any other such criterion you may find useful.

In a multi-product scenario, it always helps to have a clear-cut idea about profitability of each segment. Hence, product mix is extremely important, and it is very... very... important to market products in manner suited to a product mix. **Increase in sales means nothing if products sold are of**

less profitable nature. Quarterly targets and the review may help you to achieve what you want to, or at least to modify what is going on. Ideally each product should be able to fit in the over-all picture of total product mix. Before nay new product or a variant of an existing product is launched, be sure that you have done you homework very correctly, and projection on the scale of a maximum 20 to 25% achievement over a period of 3 years, leaves you in a comfortable position. Chances are that you may succeed if you succeed on paper, (drawing board stage). Each character should be on paper, very heavily substantiated with some solid logic, then and then only you may even think f test marketing and test launch.

2. Output Goals – Once the product goals are decided and accepted, the next logical step is to decide on the optimal output goals. Can you produce the optimal quantity at an optimal price for an optimal period of time on constant basis? Do you have the required infrastructure to produce and more importantly to market? If no, how soon can you get it? On a pre-decided time- frame, you have to seriously answer these questions. It is one thing to produce goods (which in itself a big achievement), but it is absolutely important to market these goods, at a pre-decided profit margin. Are you aware about the variables, in terms of consumer behavior, government rules and regulations or their changes? Are you sure that these are going to be constant, at least over a period of time?

If you are supplying to, say, power industry or steel industry or textiles, have you accumulated any worthwhile data on the future status of these industries? Or you may be holding the proverbial bowl, as by the time you are ready to supply, because of 180^0 change in the status of industry as compared to "today"' and the need of your products is gone. Most of the industries in our country are victims of this situation.

3. System Goals

Any working organisation has to have a 'running' system. Most of the organisations have a vague idea about such systems in their own backyard. Because the organisation has been "working" and in some cases "generating profits" it is assumed that it is automatic. The jolt comes when things start going askew.

The manner of functioning in an organisation is the 'system'. There is no thumb rule or a readymade model available. The text book models, of top heavy or bottom-heavy type are generally helpful in doing the 'post-mortem' of a failed organisation.

Ideally you should understand that the system of functioning should be considered independent of the goods manufactured or services provided. There can be a substitution, like 'X' product for 'Y' and 'L' services of 'M'. The system developed should be able to function for all of these, without any substantial alteration.

The system should be designed for growth, stability, sustained rate of profit, span of controls, tight or loose handling, and initiative increase. Now, you will realise that for achieving these system goals your products may have a little say. So, system goals should pertain to achieving desired conditions of working in an organisation. System goals should have a holistic approach rather than based on a product or a service perspective.

As growth is more relevant to the scope of this book let us deal with growth objective in a little more detail.

Most organisations are obsessed with growth. While in a very hot pursuit of this impressive goal, most organisations tend to forget that growth is not automatic, but tends the create pain and stress. It is very important that you decide whether you want growth or profitability and high returns or your investment; along with growth. Most managers in modern era are preoccupied with growth and hence tend to overlook the other side of growth. As any other thing in life, growth also demands a cost, which many organisations are not ready to pay.

Before the advent of organized management culture, (somewhere in 1960) in our country, we had our own systems, which have been running successfully for centuries. And even today these organisations are happily living. In fact, now the formal management institutions have included curriculum designed for family businesses, (for example – S.P. Jain Institute of Management at Mumbai). Quite welcome signs.

Whenever I talked to such family-controlled businessmen as regards their plans for growth, the answer was generally same. They would like to grow provided growth does not upset their present, per-tested routines. Such units very often are in the eyes of the giants for a possible takeover bid, or growth may force them to go public, even if they would not wish to dilute their family hold and hence decision to "grow" can be really very tricky. Because once the ball is rolled in the path of growth, the process becomes irreversible, and many times poses a threat of even a closure of the unit.

Does it mean growth is something evil? No! Not at all, Growth is definitely important. It is a sure sign of success, in some cases even prestige. On the path of growth, organisations are a better place to work, where promotions are easy. As the size of operations grows, so does the size of pay-packages to senior employees.

Growth also opens doors to various fresh talents. More people from outside with specific skills can enter a growing organisation. Each new entrant also brings a part of his skill, as well as destiny to the organisation. The organisation tends to become more vibrant, more prone to changes, and welcomes new technologies.

Decision about when to grow is probably the single largest factor in the resultant success. Life is all about timing, as said by Carl Lewis, the legendary athlete from US of A. How aptly it applies in a sector totally different such as growth in an industry. In a booming economy there is ample scope of growth and everybody enjoys the benefits available at relative ease. If your growth decision should ideally match with a crest in economy, then you are in a stage of windfall. But in a faltering economy or an assumed state of depression, it takes real analysis, rather than guts, to expand.

Growth is a system goal as you can by now see, that it is what you want irrespective of the products or services you are dealing in.

5. Marketing Goals

It is very ironic in our country that the organisations do not even today, attach any importance to marketing. In fact, it is the last item or priority. So carried away people are, that their "goods" or "services" are unique, top class that they tend to forget marketing. After all, they believe (wrongly) that because their products are good – sorry – excellent, economic, they shall automatically find market. In the project reports which are made mostly by consultants who have never have sold anything in life, often they downplay this activity. More over the projections are on a hearsay rather than actual effort. The bank manager is not bothered, when he sanctions a loan depending upon such a project report. The result is the daily advertisements of closures, attachment and cases in front of Loan Recovery Tribunal.

Why this happens? Have you anytime given a thought to? Whose money is it anyway? Is the proposed industry to be set up for successful running, or, for the ever-present subsidy and tax benefits?

My experience has shown me a prototype of Indian Entrepreneurship; which seems to be pre-dominantly production oriented.

In the first case, a son a grandson in a business family is on the verge of graduation and the Karta. (Dadaji) on his own decides to set up a unit for his grandson (Lalla, Munna etc.) The readymade project report is submitted to already manipulated bank officers; loan is taken from state financial institution as well as banks. The personal stake of maximum 40% of the total project cost is already recovered by way of say subsidy, more than necessary construction, excess billing in plant and machinery, and any other available sources. Prevalent, at that particular time, even before single unit is manufactured. Nobody has given any thought to marketing. When the unit starts producing and stocks are piled up, a marketing manager is hired whose salary is always looked down upon as an unnecessary expense. Once the stocks are liquidated to a manageable level, the marketing manager is instantly replaced by some lowly paid sales representatives. (Why should we pay so much to one person, when 3 or 4 lowly paid reps can do the same thing? After all marketing does not need any intelligence or original idea) the cycle is repeated, whatever funds are generated, are fast pilfered into personal account and the unit is declared sick. After all, the unit was meant **to pay to the owners, which it has already done.**

Thankfully the present government has finally addressed to this organized crime committed by the officials and the businessmen. It has introduced a tribunal called National Company Law Tribunal. When the bankrupt unit's assets are attached to the tribunal, things become really tight for the erring business community. It is the welcome status today, but mind you, the Indian business community is very smart. It is always ahead of the government sadly, in the matter of cheating and bending the law. In the near future they would find a way to circumvent these new rules. I am sure about this fact as the stakeholders in the process are still the same old characters who are morally bankrupt and almost antinational.

In the second case it is generally an engineer who either could not get a decent job, or has worked for 3 to 5 years and suddenly finds holding a product idea, which he finds brilliant. Again, due to government policies he gets comparatively easy loans. He is very sure about the quality of his product so naturally marketing is not looked into. After all, product is so good that it should sell automatically. Again, the result is a sort of foregone conclusion and one sick unit is added to the long list.

In the third case, generally it is an ancillary unit depending heavily upon some public sector undertaking like a power plant, steel plant etc. As soon as, the parent unit in trouble, the ancillary unit follows the dreaded path of supplies without payments.

No wonder that in spite of so many assistance schemes, subsidies, easy loan, any industrial area all over the nation has a few thriving industrial units. Again, the government has schemes to revive such units, which provide one more excellent way to make some extra money for the promoters.

	High	Medium	Low
		Quality	
High Price	Premium Strategy	High Strategy	Simple Value Strategy
Medium Price	Over Charging Strategy	Medium Value Strategy	Good Value Strategy
Low Price	Rip-off Strategy	False Economy Strategy	Economy Strategy

Desired Area for Product Positioning

Product Positioning Quadrant

Product Positioning Quadrant

So, if you are an organisation who wants to survive and succeed on a long- term basis you should have a clear-cut idea about marketing in general and as regards your product proposal in specific. Apart from all the marketing terms, jargon the concerned executive, should have a simplified way of checking and cross-checking marketing process in his company.

You may be are able do decide your marketing goals very neatly if you study following and are able to position your product correctly.

Second chart you should seriously study is:

	New Area	Old Area
New Product	**NPNA** Launch of New Product / Concept	Consolidation of Good will **NPOA**
Old Product	New Market (Expansion **OPNM**	Usual Hard work Back breaking **OPOA**

Product positioning Quadrant

In these two charts you can fit in any product and have some success. The efforts for each of the motive are specific and results are generally positive. It may appear over-simplified but it works.

I can not give any ready-made idea to derive on marketing goals because I want you to think study and then decide your own goals and more importantly work very hard to achieve them.

Social Goals:

Every other animal except for **Homo sapiens,** live without probably attaching any significance to the same. (The statement may hurt some intelligent animals, if only they can read.) That animals have some social systems is evident from the research and is an accepted fact in case of elephants, honeybees etc.

A human being is different and tries to live his life in pre-determined rules, as and when the rules suit, and in some cases profitable. Whenever we try to discuss society, we should separate the aspect of money from "society". The results with or without money are absolutely striking and, in some cases, can be an eye opener for many of us.

Ideally social goal should be very easy to define, but in practice, talking of social goals is sort of a fuzzy logic. All the talk of social up liftment and social quality has been nothing but a lot of hot air. And presently in India it has crossed all the limits of insanity. Sadly, the leadership, if it can be called so, has no inking of this subject. Ironically, there is no qualification, no practice or fro that matter decency, is a pre-requisite to launch yourself in "**leadership**" business. Whenever this work leadership is mentioned, one should exclude **political leadership** from the same then and then probably some sensible discussion can be possible, at least in present scenario.

Leadership As I Perceive:

I have been very critical of the leadership that is presently available or not available in India. I have a feeling that similar situation should be prevalent in the rest of world also. The selfless leadership is probably a thing of ancient era.

The criticism concerns mainly those leaders who may not be 'leaders' in the true sense of the word. The political leadership to the Netagiri is the one, I am seriously worried about.

Ideally, the leadership should decide the aspirations, the goals of any organisation, or even a nation. For this, the vision becomes the foremost and critical component.

I have divided leadership into following and shall try to discuss same in very short:
- Organisational Leadership
- Political Leadership
- Social Leadership

Organisation Leadership

Fortunately, we have very strong family bond, in most of the fore-runners in Industrial sector, in India. Whenever, we name any industry such as Bajaj, Reliance, Mahindra and Mahindra, Videocon, Tatas, Birla's, Escorts, JK Group, Wipro, we are certain to find, that family plays a major role. Because of the involvement of family and family-oriented objectives, somethings such as loyalty, sincerity, integrity are automatically taken care of. The leadership may or may not commit mistakes, but the intention can never be in doubt. So many success stories are available to choose from, that every Indian should feel safe and proud. All the gentlemen, who control their organisations with such a wide base and varying styles, that it should be a very obvious topic of management research. The comprehension of economic condition, its effects, and how to make most of it, is quite complete in the minds of the organizational leaders.

Mr. Azim Premji, the Chairman of Wipro Group, in his valedictory address, at the convocation, at IIM, Ahmedabad, has been very wonderful. He has discussed the changes and management of changes, in a candid way. (The address is available on net; it you want to read)

No wonder that the industries are looking up and may be in the next decade or so, we may be very near to the required levels of development and growth.

Political Leadership

I am sure that this is the problem area, in our country. In fact, if there is even a **marginal improvement**, in this very haphazardly handled are, we can zoom into a **very bright future**.

Political leadership, to me, is the most vital part in the development of any country. People, self-proclaimed leaders, leaders, in the accepted term and political thinkers have a definite role to play in this function. For understanding this concept of political leadership, let us try to classify it.

In India, political leadership can be, divided into

- Neta
- Political (leaders) or Politicians
- Statesman

Neta - In the school or college, the "netas" (may be 6 out of 10) are sadly, the bully types, of the college. Because of his physical might, in some cases, coupled with the relationship with political leader, such a person can be t the helm of affairs, as he can afford to spend money. The other students, who are more pre-occupied with their studies, exams, treat these 'Netas' as a nuisance. Probably it is here that the beginning of unwanted divide can be traced to. It is here the more nature, more thinking students decide, that politics is for the "vagabonds". Once this is done, such a decision is kept valid for the rest of their lives. And they begin a lifelong "watching" of things going wrong, and keep criticizing, but feel that they cannot do anything. The irony is those **who can think, do not do anything worthwhile**, but those **who cannot think** unfortunately **do many things**, most of which cause **irreversible damage** to the **image of the country.**

These 'netas' once out of the colleges, (if they go to), start their 'political neatagiri', by becoming handymen of their earlier generation, who have by now become corporators, MLAs, MLCs or even MPs. The vicious circle is going on and the standard is going downwards, on a daily basis. It is probably at this stage all the "would be" Netas learn that the law and law enforcing authorities can be suitably manipulated with a principle of money and "mobbocracy". Moreover the "leaders" under whom, these would be 'nets' take their training, sadly do not have anyting worthwhile to teach. It is here they get the unnecessary training of money and muscle power, using which they learn the art of manipulation, falsification, pseudo sweet talk, booth capturing and more recently, even the kidnapping, ransom etc.

It is here we Indian have to unite against such useless and harmful mobs, if we have to live in peace and harmony, in the near future.

Political Leadership or Politicians

From a very long time in history politicians have been defined very appropriately. I need not go into them. You know and you have been enjoying the definitions.

Being a politician, it the only profession, where there is no defined requirement of qualification, experience or even the attributes.

Also, it is an easy profession if you know how to handle the population, that is the sentiment of the people. Moreover, people when see a politician, they automatically accept his corruption immoral practices. It is in fact they have come to understand, that politics is necessarily business of such people only. This is a very sad state of affairs and has to change very fast.

Divide and rule is what the Britishers have taught, but even the Britishers shall also be astonished to note the expertise acquired by our politicians. The politicians have divided our country on a regional, lingual, religion basis, communal basis, labor unions, caste basis, north-south, east-west basis, rich and poor basis, male-female basis, educated-uneducated basis, employed-unemployed basis, and as if these divides are not enough our politicians are working overtime to research all those new areas, on the basis of which further divisions shall be possible.

Why I say that this business of politics is easy? Because if you see the voting percentage in our country, you shall be surprised to note that it revolves round 50% mark. This means that the other 50% are either not interested in what happens to their country or they are convinced that nothing is going to change. The results on the basis of 50%, go to elect people, who rule 100%. This is the reason why I feel that to win a election the candidate must have 51% of votes of the total votes and not the cotes polled. This single step can ascertain a sensible scenario.

Politicians who are elected on the basis of a mere _headcount can never do anything worthwhile_, as has been evident over a period last 6 decades. That, if India has developed or achieved some progress, it is definitely, in spite of politicians, rather than because of them.

Statesman – Once, in a debate, at one of the conferences, a question was put to all of us, the delegates. The question was "What is the difference between a politician and statesman?" One person answered and his answer probably, sums up. He said "In a case of statesman, "man" is still alive, where as in a politician no "man" exists."

Statesman type, leadership is what our country today needs. Statesmen are normally accepted as stately, dignified and thoughtful. They are supposed to have some expertise, in at least a field or two.

Fortunately, even today, India has such leadership, albeit on a lesser scale. Further, it is very welcome fact that these statesmen are present in each and every political party. And it is these people, even though in a distinct minority, the country looks up to, to rectify the situation.

The statesmen if can look into the future, share their vision control the unruly elements in their respective party shall, do a tremendous job for the betterment of the country. They should also remember that they are the "men" of "the state", and behave accordingly.

Social Leadership

Social leadership in our country can be traced back to times immemorable. All the social reforms, which were possible, are mainly due to these people, who selflessly worked for the upliftment of society. What they did was impeccable, but what their followers are doing today needs a close scrutiny.

It is in this field we have an aura of leadership. Be it, Gandhiji, Veer Savarkar, Swami Vivekananda, Mother Teresa, Fule, Ambedkar, Agarkar, Raja Ram Mohan Roy, and so many others, everyone of them has contributed to uplift the social harmony.

There are so many social leaders in each state, who have contributed, but are out of limelight. NGOs, who are sincere in their pursuit of objectives, have contributed immensely in fields where the slow speed of government agencies, makes it impossible to reach. Social leadership is more difficult, because social leaders generally survive solely on the basis of what they actually do, rather than any other clout or influence. They are leaders, because of the people they serve, think so.

My only wish is that this selfless servant leadership should continue to exist and help the nation to build it image correctly.

In the last decade or so, it was very fashionable to project and organisation with a social objective. You shall recall "We also make steel", type slogans, from this period. "Desh ki Dhadkan" etc. is all very confusing. Socio economic parameters have never been clear and shall never be. In fact, if an organisation, one with manufacturing and selling functions, starts talking about social services it sure is a signal of alarm. Tobacco companies, wine and liquor companies, can keep spending billions in any currency prevalent in the world for the promotions, but we the people must remember that each unit of such currency unit has been generated in a questionable social manner. It is like the very often proclaimed truth in the Hindu religion. The <u>origin</u> of food one eats, the <u>origin</u> of money one spends, has a very permanent <u>impact</u> on the overall thought process of the concerned human being.

"Is my organisation doing anything for the society about which I should be proud of?" should be the question every thinking organizer should ask of himself very frequently. If the answer is towards negative, then he should do the required correction, towards evolving such a product line, or working system. The more the organisation starts to hide behind various readymade excuses, media hypes, the more uncomfortable, they become. The slide has already begun, even if presently, you are minting money. Making money and having a worthwhile organisation of which you and your nation can be proud of, are two altogether different things. Is your money a product of something evil? If yes, why do you have to have such money, what are the compulsions which you cannot get rid of, shall ultimately answer you about your social responsibility (it you are willing to) and subsequent accomplishment of any such goal.

While deciding social goals the organisations are very often use ornate language, which, though impressive has very little truth in it. Hence before setting up any social goal the organisation must answer this question very sincerely and truthfully. "What business are you in?" Spend some time before your answer. The guideline to be used in similar to the one used by good police officers or detective. **Don't fall for the obvious.** "Think" is a keyword.

To me any social goals before operational excellence is like the proverbial horse, and the cart. To have a social goal is one thing and to have resources on a continuous basis to fulfill the goals is altogether different. The gradual stages in life of a man also say, something. First learn, ten apply, earn some money, they spend. Some religions have even a clear-cut instruction on this line, if you care to look for them

Peter Drucker, the management guru, in his book ("The Practice of Management" page no.390) says, "It is management's responsibility to make whatever is generally in the public good, to become the entrepreneur's own self-interest. He further says "There is a responsibility of management to the public interest as such. This is based on the fact that the enterprise is an organ of the society."

My teacher at Sydenham College, Mumbai used to say that the basic purpose any commercial operation should be to serve the needs of people, albeit, at an accepted rate of profit.

The relationship of the society and any enterprise is multi-facial and can be quite complex. The society is the one who pays ultimately, both in cases of either success or failure of an enterprise. Any new idea has always benefited the society and the cost benefit analysis is automatically worked out by the paying customers in the society, before accepting or rejecting the idea or concept. Plastics, telephones, internet, computers and many such concepts have passed this acid test in a very convincing way.

In this context, when an organisation is making money from the society, of which the organisation is itself, a small or big part, depending upon the turnover, has to pay back in decent way. This notion should be an ideal basis for a social goal in the organisation. The programmer which should be conducted by the leading lights of such as operating organisation should be well thought, and should be in the step with the society. Upliftment of cultural values, helping out a sports activity, providing facility of education to needy students, conducting correct training programs, sponsoring a town or village, helping hand for the health activity, can be some of the ideal social goals. All such activity not only creates a pleasant ambience but also opens doors to overall upliftment and development of the area, in which the organisation is functioning.

But it should be prudent here to remind the organisation decision makers that these goals towards the society should be always accepted as secondary and more importantly it should be certainly ascertained that these goals, are not achieved at the cost of the society itself. If such is a case the basic purpose of having such a goal is defeated. If the prices are to be hiked, after every such event or activity, then it is felt that it should be much better to drop them, and keep giving the product at the same cost, which anyway shall constitute as the best service to the society.

***

CHAPTER SIX

Stress of Growth

Stress of Growth

As has been already said most of us take growth as an automatic process. Once the process is considered in this perspective, it is very easy to forget the effects and after effects of growth. A company, with a turnover of Rs. 1 crore, suddenly gets a huge order of Rs. 10 crores, is very happy. After the initial euphoria the truth starts to sink in. Most companies may have made a total mess of the order and some of the very few who fulfill the order, within prescribed time frame, shall certainly relate with this term 'Stress of Growth'. By the time the order is over, very few in the company are able to retain their cheerful attitude. During this vital period, all the weak links in the organisation are exposed very badly, and the Chief Executives start worrying about how they could have carried so many passengers. The elastic limits are tested causing a great stress all though the left, right and centre of the organisation.

On a personal level a person who gets a promotion before he is ready, experiences the same anxiety and the stress. He may accept the same or not, is another thing. A very common example is available in banking sector. A person handling the cash and only cash in a bank generally finds promotions extremely hot, when promoted and is supposed to handle all functions in the banking activity, of which he has no idea or working experience.

A frontline salesman when promoted to a supervisory position finds it difficult and very stressful because of

a) Reduction in income, by way of less TA / DA

b) He has no inkling about how to manage his juniors. He may know how to work himself, but cannot transfer his knowledge of his juniors and get the work done.

So, any person should seriously think about his growth, whether he can cope up or not? To understand the relationship between growth and its stress, we have to find meaning of stress.

Stress can be defined as an imbalance in the system, due to permanent presence of factors that cause strain. Strain is a result of singular, strain in due to temporary situations that originate duet o certain tensions, or abnormal situations if life. But strain on physical or mental faculties of humans, on a continuous basis ultimately results in stress. Anger, tensions without possible solutions, frustrations, inability to do things right on a prolonged basis cause stress. When stress persists over a period of time it causes physical and /or psychological disorders. Most of the times a person becomes aware of this stage and starts a backward journey to regain the earlier stage of equilibrium.

Stress is a phenomenon which affects human beings ironically even in happiness, contrary to the general belief. Happy emotional imbalances also cause stress, like winning a bumper lottery prize, though more manageable as compared to the stress effected by unhappy situations. On this basis, stress is divided into two major categories Eustress and Distress.

Eustress is caused by excess of joy, or a positive impulse due to sports, hobbies, or even sex. As an industrialist or an entrepreneur or an executive stress can be in form of an opportunity, which enhances the scope of working, stretches the person to the limits, earlier unknown to him and if he sustains and survives, he can be successful, and may enjoy, the benefits.

Distress is usually more known and more talked about from of stress. Psychologists and psychotherapists have been fighting this very damaging, but most of the times invisible disease, over decades. Distress is also more destructive as compared to Eustress. Distress produces unpleasant conditions due to continuous psychological or physical strain of various kinds.

Both conditions of eustress and distress, is extreme, can be very dangerous to the human beings.

Stress is identified to occur on a physical and /or psychological level. Both are created due to an immense demand on the physiology of human beings. Physical stress is more direct and identifiable. Examples are accidents, major and minor surgeries, infections, injuries and most horrible injuries, due to burns. Psychological stress can be either in isolation or in association and /or reaction of physical stress. The seven bad characters can be very well identified with psychological stress, Jealousy, anger, fear, worry, excess of pride, excess of sex, hatred, conflicts on conscious as well as sub-conscious levels are few examples. (As also seven sins in the Bible)

Stress is caused on a temporary basis for example when you experience very bad nightmare the stress is almost real, but temporary, as when you are awake it is gone. Or when you slip on a polished floor, you feel a shock, it may hurt you physically, but if you slip in public, it hurts your pride also, again on a temporary basis. As soon as you get up, you tend to rebound to your normal routine.

On a permanent basis stress may cause damages such as manias, bipolar manic depressions and even more severe reactions causing permanent imbalance, leading to lunatic asylum.

To understand the relationship between strain and stress, let me give you a very common example. A thin metal wire when folded abruptly undergoes a strain, but is in a position to regain its properties. But when exposed to this strain on a repeated basis, it finally breaks and undergoes an irreversible damage. You can apply same situation in cases of human beings, institutions, organisations and nations.

Why stress occurs? What is the origin of this dreaded ailment? How desire to grow affects us? Does stress have something to do, with the childhood circumstances, lousy parenting, and fierce competition. Maybe, yes!

In a present-day world, where materialistic approach rules, the emphasis is on more speed, more efficiency, more product ion, more ruthless evaluation, more competition and so many other such factors, each causing a tension. To cope up with the expectation of parents, teachers, employees, relatives and society in general, common man tends to overwork himself. To reach the summit of super exportations and norms, living standards, he keeps on stretching himself so much so that he does not have time to look back. He does not care or can not find a moment, of rest for his withering body.

A typical businessman of today has to attend, so many varied stress causing situations in a day. Further worse is that he can not afford to show that is under strain of any kind. As the excited emotions cannot find a way out, due to a typical "stiff upper lip" pre-condition, it leads to very serious inner conflicts. The solution lies in getting away for a while, which he can ill afford to, so he goes for medical assistance, gets prescribed some medicines (anti depressants etc.), further continues to work like a "donkey". All this effort, if met with success is worth (?) the stress caused or otherwise as prevalent today may result in suicides, which **any way is a permanent solution to a temporary problem.**

The man today flies faster than the speed of sound, has conquered the power of an atom, has achieved miracles in medical science, surpassed all earlier ideas of production, communication, technology, outer space, yet, when it comes to the inner sanctorum of mind, he finds himself to be deficient on many accounts. In spite of all technology and its advantages man has yet not found universally accepted way of life which will allow him to live in peace, along with his neighboring country.

I always say that world could have been very peaceful, following the rules of nature; before the advent of man. When we see the world, we find that most reasons of friction are manmade. (Religion, Money, Marriage, Makeup, Nations, Maps, Community). The basic reason the man creates imbalance is due to his insecurity. He does not accept rules of nature. He starts to store more that he needs and then holds the other faction of humanity to a ransom. To protect himself from the unknown, he keeps on producing weapons of mass destruction, which he knows, he may never use.

So, the pertinent question one must answer is: are the developed, really "developed?" Are we better than our forefathers who were more at peace with them selves or more "Grown up" than us, the present-day lot? On a holistic scale can we really say that we are better?

Along with our growth, we face two major challenges in absolutely unrelated areas, the first is pollution. Waste management, noise pollution, emission exhausts, radiation wastes, oil spillovers is oceans, forest firs, mine fires, synthetic milk, organic food, are the areas which need our immediate attention, if we have to survive.

The second challenge is stress. In spite of the intentional goose chase for development and some results, which may be worthwhile, mankind finds, itself stranded hopelessly when faced with increasing unemployment, health hazards (aids, cancer, malaria, dengue), decreasing quality of life (without peace and serenity), social unrest, student unrest, decreasing moral values resulting in corruption, extra marital affairs, divorces, increasing suicide percentages. Industrial espionage, organized crime, utter disregard for intellectual property, piracy, yellow journalism. The efforts of mankind to find solutions to these problems can be at best compared with a cat trying to catch its won tail. In spite of the huge amounts spent on stress management the results are meager. Mankind has yet to understand one basic rule that "too much too soon without efforts" is not possible.

So, after all this, you still want to pursue growth? You are right in doing so. You should analyse the reasons for such a situation wherein you want to grow and find yourself exerting, with no visible results. You should study such factors very... very carefully before you decide to grow.

Is it possible that you grow without appreciable stress and pain? Is it possible that you manage to grow and still maintain cheerful attitudes towards you work? How positive attitudes can help you? Is money, very important in the process of growth? You should ask such questions to yourself and try to find answers suitable to your situations.

***

CHAPTER SEVEN

Growth Without Pain?

Growth Without Pain?

Yes, it is possible! And you will be, probably, pleasantly surprised if you know that it is up to you and you alone, to achieve, such a miracle.

Pain generally arises from the fact that you do anything without liking it. It is also associated with all those unwanted things you come across in your life. Pain from physical injuries is manageable with treatment and medicines, as against injury to human pride, which tends to remain aggravated throughout the remaining life. Physical injuries get healed, may be, they leave a scar, as a faint reminder of the agony, you suffered, but not so in case of injured pride. In case of physical injury, after it is healed it can no longer cause an iota of pain, you earlier suffered, but injured pride has a potent capacity to cause increasing agony, every next time, you reminded of it. They have a great potential to turn physical, when they persist over a period of time. A single derogatory laugh caused the greatest war, (Mahabharat). So, please understand the power of pain.

The real pleasure of proper growth probably originates from the fact the one has grown and reached a predetermined destination with all possible co-ordinates, fighting his way out of the trouble. In spite of proper planning every project has some factors which are capable of creating a threat to the very existence of the project. Ask any successful person, he should have a story or two to narrate.

So, in spite of all such hue and cry regarding the inhibitors of growth why everyone is willing to grow? There are some who grow, and others, who do not achieve what they would have. What is difference? Is it something to do with attitude, aptitude, available inputs or is it something different?

Let us try to find out.

(1) You should know that growth in a natural and normal way, may not cause any stress, but it may not produce desired prosperity and affluence.

You have to stretch much beyond your accepted and existing capacity to achieve additional growth in the same frame of time.

So, the question is "Are you ready for the extra effort?"

(2) The pain comes from doing things which you do not like. Any growth under any unwanted pressure or coercion is not worthwhile. The decision to grow has to be voluntary. **Ideally you say "I do because I want to".**

(3) The desire to grow in itself does not assure any results. But this decision and its power should not be underestimated. In most of the cases the decision itself does not take place, which ultimately blocks all roads leading to growth.

(4) Once the decision is taken to achieve "something" (in the actual case it should be very specifically defined in terms of volume, size, time etc.) You should not waver from it. Most of the times, we find that we compromise and are very willing to lower the bar, to more "acceptable" levels. We have to replace "impossible" with "may be at present improbable."

(5) All talks of positive thinking alone cannot achieve anything. Positive thinking is a must, but it has to be in association of a concrete action. Norman Vincent Peale, the original thinker, who coined the phrase "The poser of positive thinking" in the early fifties, says in his book. (Why some positive thinkers get powerful results?)

Think positively

<u>Act positively</u>

Image positively to get positive results

Pray positively

& Believe positively

There is nothing said about "talk positively" Mere positive talking is not enough. It can not move even a blade of grass.

It is very fashionable these days to talk about positive thinking. Let us analyse the positive thinking in the Current Indian Environment. If positive thinking is accepting whatever the boss or the minister says, many Indians are master positive thinkers. These Indian are also known as "Chamchas", a very prolific community growing faster than the congress grass **(Parthenium).**

To me positive thinking is considering all aspects with regard to any project under scrutiny. Why it will succeed or are there any reasons which may make the project unsuccessful? It always pays rich dividends, if you know in advance, about things which may go wrong. You may even cancel or postpone the initiation, try to find out suitable plan (A), (B) or even (C).

All projects which are conceived may not look as promising, when seen under a proverbial microscope. Nothing wrong in it, when you are in a position to accept or reject a proposal, on a drawing board stage, you are fortunate, as you have not incurred any const on it. So long as you have some more projects lined up, it really should not matter.

(6) Once decision has been taken you should be very careful. The first thing you should do is to take a realistic stock of available resources. And, as it is universally accepted the first resource is the 'men' around you. Try to pick from your existing group, the few who think like you, have capacity to stretch or go for a logical hunt. Remember you alone can not do everything, so you would need people. Get some commitment. Do not compromise on this account.

(7) Always talk about rewards well in advance vis a vis the achievements. And in the future honor your commitments. Awards promised and not give, (as is the case in many Indian Industries) can erode your credibility, beyond any repairs.

(8) Learn to appreciate. This single act of yours can compensate for many of your other shortcomings. Correct appreciation, at a correct time, can motivate a person to perform beyond his limits.

(9) Periodic reviews are a must if you want to keep the project on track.

(10) Like most visionaries, you should be ready with a new project idea, by the time the current project is heading towards the successful conclusion.

If you manage to do and monitor your growth project in the above fashion, you may find that growth is comparatively less painful.

***

Monitoring Growth

Monitoring Growth

Monitoring any ongoing process is very vital, because it may emerge as a single factor that influences the process, and to ensure the success. Any manager shall tell you that an excellent plan without proper monitoring can fall apart in no time. On a day-to-day basis monitoring, can be very reassuring as it tells you whether or not you are on a right path to success. Monitoring ensures correct implementation, which is the key to success.

We all know that enacting a law is not by itself enough to deliver results; it is to be very ably supported by implementation. Even an organisation of the level of a senate or parliament finds itself helpless to enforce the law, unless it is willing to work overtime for correct implementations.

Monitoring is an easy process provided it is done on a day-to-day basis. Any backlog on this account is usually fatal for the projects.

After a lot of deliberation following format has been designed as a general guideline to all those who are inclined towards proper growth appraisal, which is suitable for an organization.

MONITORING MODEL FOR AN ORGANISATION

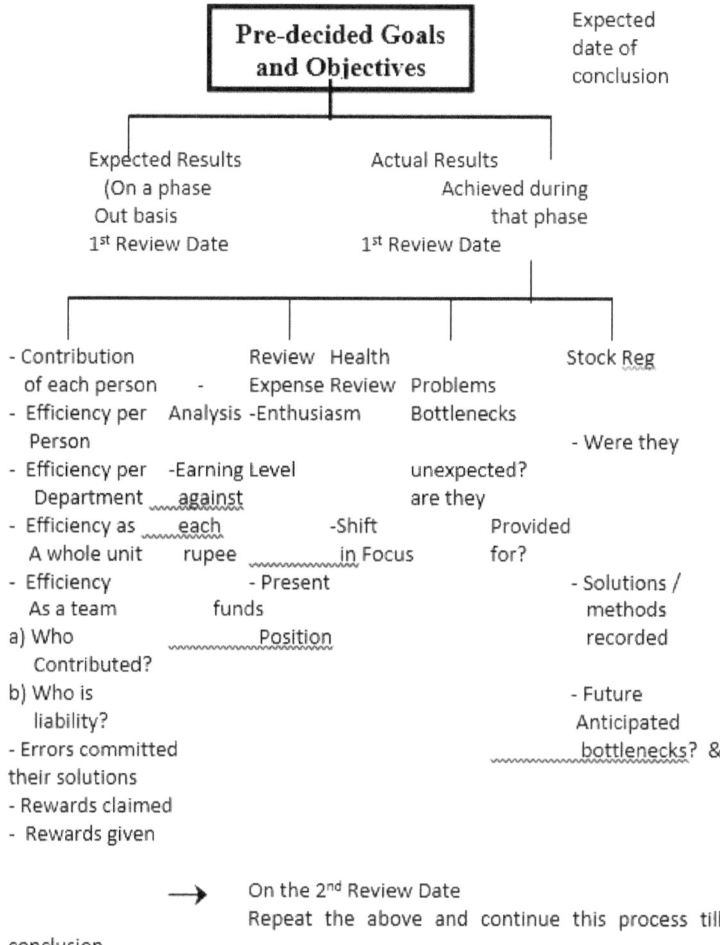

MONITORING MODEL FOR AN ORGANISATION

As a person who knows his job best, you may add a perspective here and there, in this format.

While operating on this model some basic things are to be always kept in mind.

(1) The first one is that leader has to be very firm in his commitment. He should know what he wants and more importantly he should be able

to transfer his vision on a continuous basis. Most importantly he should be able to keep the spirits of 'his' team 'up' throughout the operating period of the project.

(2) The evaluation process should be similar to all concerned. The techniques used should be as clear as possible, so that feeling of injustice to any one is avoided. Also, in such cases the comparisons are more worthwhile.

(3) The third and probably most important is proper way of appreciation. The rule to be followed is "Recognition in Public, Censure in Private."

Public dressing down has been a biggest and probably single largest reason for the sagging spirits and fall in performance.

The project leader should be innovative enough to find out ways of recognizing his people for their performance. Timely recognitions with limited fanfare are the best booster doses, so necessary for an ongoing rigorous project.

Coming back to our model for monitoring growth, I feel that the model and features are very simple and almost self0explanatory. And it shall be a fun if you find out what suits you or a not, and modify this prototype as per your requirements.

Think about following questions. They may help you in better monitoring.

- Why should any customer select your organisation for his operations?
- What different facilities, can you provide which are unique?
- If all the organisations are controlled by Central Govt. Policies/or by Co-operative Department's Guidelines, what is special about your own organisation?
- When the customer walks into your premises do you see him as a life time partner in your business or just another nuisance?
- Does your organisation give an impression as well – oiled smooth-running machine?
- Do you need "May I help you on the counters or each person in your organisation has a helping attitude towards customer?
- How do you rate service offered by your organisation? Is it good or can it be improved?
- What do you feel about the goodwill of your organisation?

- What is the level of motivation? Is your staff happy? Does the happiness show on their faces when they attend the customers?
- Do you have a sense of belonging? If, yes, have you been able to transfer the same to your staff?
- Just imagine that a chairman of a very huge group of companies walks into your organisation, are you equipped to service the needs of his organisations. If yes, can you list your positives? If no, can you find out what extra efforts are needed?
- Would you prefer your organisation for your own operations, if you were to start a new business?
- If you are given the absolute powers to govern your organization, would you continue to follow the same policies, methods or seek some changes? If no, why? If yes, what are those changes?
- At the end of each day are you sure that you have given your best effort to your organisation? Can you recall how many days in the recent past you had a similar feeling?

<u>Monitoring on Personal Level</u>

Monitoring on a personal level can be easy or very difficult depending upon what type of person you are. If you understand that you can not cheat your conscience or the inner self, you stand a good chance of getting self-monitored; in a profitable way.

Again, the first step is to decide the purpose of any act. If you aim at wrong goal, you definitely shall miss it. You have to think, imagine and then physically act. I shall give you some examples to explain my viewpoint.

Sometime ago a young man approached are for advice regarding his career. He was a graduate engineer, and after his graduation, was trying to find a worthwhile occupation. On the day of our meeting, he had received a call letter, for an entrance test, in an information technology giant company. During the discussion, I asked him as to why he wanted to go to Bangalore, and his answer was to <u>appear for the exam</u>. As in the case of most 'non-thinking' people, his response was OK, but was it a correct goal or reason? I feel he would have been better placed of he was gong to Bangalore, to <u>get the particular job</u>. That to get the sought-after job, he would have to appear for a test, group discussion or at the end appear for a personal interview. But in all such situations his goal would have been constant, that is to get the job. I suggested him to fine tune his reason, and within minutes, he said that he felt better.

The second situation, involves sales people throughout the world. In the daily sales report of all companies there is a column for 'purpose' of visit. Most salesmen, who are not very successful, visit customers for "Demonstration", or "Follow up". Their purpose is limited, and they go and get what they had aimed for. They get a demo, or a follow up and happily come back; without even mentioning about orders.

Where as, ideally his purpose should be to get an order or to collect payment which form the two extreme activities of a sales process. I had always found that it helps to remind myself, the purpose of my visit, just before I entered the premises of the would-be customer, such as

(a) I am here to get an order for product X, (b) quantity Y, (c) payment terms Z.

During the subsequent discussions, these a-b-c formed a suitable script and more often than not the purpose was achieved.

Once the reason or purpose is correctly decided, in any walk of life, the correct monitoring forms a backbone of your success. Your activity on a daily basis. Big question is "Do you have fifteen minutes for yourself?" When was the last time you thought exclusively about yourself for fifteen minutes? If you find this question as an irritant, you are in company of many other such people, who are surprised to note that it was probably months, if not years, when they last thought about themselves, in a serious manner. If you are not interested in yourself, why the world should be interested in you? The usual answer doled out is lack of time, which again is a lot of crap.

A mirror can be a very useful tool, in improving this situation. Before you begin your day, stand in front of a mirror, and tell yourself your daily routine. What are those 3 things which you would be doing in the course of the day, tell the mirror, when you come back, just before retiring to sleep, again stand in front of the mirror and report your achievements or reasons for not achieving, the pre-decided self-said things. Within a span of fifteen days, you shall find yourself much better organized, and full of spirits.

If you somehow, find a way to cheat the mirror then God help you.

Just before you got o sleep, before you shut your eyes ask yourself a very vital question to monitor yourself.

Am I better than yesterday?

***

Monitoring on a National Level:

On a national level monitoring growth is very difficult because the parameters themselves are beyond comprehension of most of us. The GDP, the sensex, the wholesale price index, Index numbers, the SLR, the rate of inflation, are things which are parroted by all the news channels mean hardly anything to the common man, who, without realizing is paying for all these fanfares. What you cannot imagine, you cannot improve. You cannot think about monitoring. The expression of the anchor on the telecast, says it all. In his mind he certainly has the "Better than thou" attitude.

To monitor the growth of any nation there is a house; either elected or selected members occupying it, spending money of a common man. These houses have become probably biggest con game houses, all over the world. What they do inside and outside of this house is of least concern of these 'servants' of people. In fact, the word has a lopsided meaning now. If you still have any questions about this, please view a direct telecast of question hour, on any working day of parliament in session.

Whenever, a question is asked about progress of any project, the concerned minister rises and doles out figures, not of completion of a project or phases, but very strangely of the money spent, on the project. This is a big joke. If he was to answer in same way, in front of any CEO or CMD of a private sector he is assured of a proverbial kick in the back. The expression of the minister is so victorious in saying that so much money has been spent, as if spending money is very difficult. He is very "truthful" in what he answers. His departments have spent "money". Did they say anything about finishing the task? No, not at all!

Is it any wonder that we are suffering very badly at the hands of such politicians and bureaucrats? In fact, a question has always been haunting me, ever since I could think about all such things. The question is "If IASs and MBAs were and are good, why India suffers?"

Now if you feel "India is where it should be" then probably you have stopped thinking.

Compare our country with Israel and you will see the light. Countries like Japan (totally washed out in 1945) Germany have once again bounced and matter a lot in the scenario of the world economics, as against other countries.

Israel was formed in May 1948, by the exodus of the Jews from all over the world. They had no common language, no common land, no common history, but they came together and have stayed together in spite of extremely hostile neighbors. As if all these limitations were not enough, their own country presented them a very low-quality agricultural soil, scarcity of water, very harsh climate. But today after approximately same number of years of independence Israel presents a better picture. As an acknowledged expert in diamonds, drip irrigation, de-salination it commands a position which attracts premium on each of the product in produces.

Hebrew, which was considered as dead as Latin, has been revived and is operative in Israel. Why and how could the Jews do it? This is a question, which is to be answered by each and every Indian, who loves his country.

In spite of the meager resources, harsh climate, ethnic problems, constant fear of attacks due to a vulnerable international border, Israel still has some things for which all its citizens can be proud of.

As against this backdrop, India has always been very rich in natural resources, adequate rainfall, very productive soil, and a great philosophy to fall back upon and even then, we all know that India suffers.

Broadly speaking IAS and their allied services are responsible for the administration in government and the MBAs are supposed to run the show in private sector. The state of the government, I need not go into details, as every common man knows. The industries are in none too different condition ever since. MBAs have come on to the scene. The education and experience of these "more than equals" is more often than not utilized, in giving better explanations for their failures.

Where is the accountability? For al the decisions which were taken, after a lot of deliberations, started with a lot of fanfare, are in most cases in doldrums. Who bears the cost? Of course, you and me! I do not remember hearing or reading of any arrests of any IAS / IPS officers in the last 50 years. In fact, it is sadly observed, that more the corruption, more are the chances that involved officers, politicians going scot-free.

What is the perception of common man about following departments should be the real indicator of the state of affairs; I invite you as common Indian citizen to evaluate.

Department	Corrupt	Non-Corrupt	Efficient
PWD			
CPWD			
Railway			
Milk Schemes			
Police			
Excise & Customs			
Excise & Prohibition			
Public Sector Banks			
Co-op. Banks			
Social Welfare			
Education			
Industries			
Travel / Tourism			
Transport facility			
Health facility			
Stock Exchange			
Defense Service			
Judiciary			
Municipal Corporations			
Housing Boards and development boards			
Newspapers			
TV & E-Media			
Sports Control Authority.			

Perception of a comon man

You can add as many more names as you want and then put your own rating about all these department.

As regards the private industries you can select any 50 leaders and put them to your own testing and you will know the truth for yourself.

India suffers because ---

- Everybody knows everything and nobody knows anything. India suffers at the hands of officers, politicians, industrialists, touts, because we Indians have a very high level of tolerance. We have accepted that corruption and ill treatment is our fate. If once in a while we come across any exception, we are pleasantly surprised.

- India suffers because even today an average Indian is not aware about his rights and powers. People in power go out of their way to ensure that such a situation to continue, as it suits them.
- India suffers because even after nearly seven decades we do not call over selves Indians. We are Assamese, Bengalis, Biharis, Marathi, Telugu, Tamil, Kanadi, Punjabis, Sindhis, Gujaratis, much Before we are Indian. We suffer because, we never analyse what stops us from standing erect when our national anthem is on.
- India suffers because we have not whole heartedly accepted any language as a National Language.
- India suffers because even today we accept any tinpot foreign goods as better choice than our own.
- India suffers because the younger generation is unable to identify itself with India.
- India suffers because we refuse to learn our lessons from history.
- India suffers because our history is not written by an Indian. We copy and accept the history written by foreigners, who had definite vested interests in distorting the facts.
- India suffers because of defeatist attitudes. How otherwise you can explain, that at no time in the British rule, there were never more than 30000 Britishers, who could easily rule 30, 00, 00,000 (30 Crores) Indians. Today about 30000, which include lousy politicians, touts, and criminals, rule India and we accept.
- India suffers because Indians are indifferent to themselves and their fate. They are indifferent towards the Billions of rupees spent on useless projects. Because we do not think that the money belongs to us. Very conveniently we blame the government and relapse into watching the TV shows. We are callously indifferent towards the leaders, bureaucrats and managers who squander "our" money.
- India suffers because we focus on wrong things, such as religions, languages, caste geographical divides.
- India suffers because of the lack any worthwhile leadership. In the span of 1850 to 1950, India produced leaders in every walk of life. Politics, sports, science, music, arts and literature, cinema, patriots, you name it and you can at least remember 10 persons n each category, without any effort. Try doing so, since 196-, and you will know what I am talking

about. Why such bankruptcy? Have we Indians suddenly become dull? Think about it.

Even since I remember listening to political leaders, they have been shouting hoarse about caste, and casteism. They always said that they want casteless society. Equality to all is what they preach. But in practice it is not so. If you have done away with the caste, <u>**you should have removed the column of caste, sub caste, religion, etc, from at least government forms, long back. Let everyone write himself as an Indian**</u>. Why there is a rat race amongst, the leaders to include their caste in the category called reserved. Has anybody given any thought to the repercussions we are likely to suffer in the future? Unity in diversity is it real, or just another <u>threadbare cliché.</u>

India suffers because average Indian hardly knows about national pride, along with so many other things. It is really unfortunate situation that even after six decades of independence, the politicians, the bureaucrats, the managers, the teachers, the coaches, are unable to instill one simple thing in the minds of Indians, that they are Indians, and they should be proud to be so.

The above account should be a sufficient report card for most of us. Let us spend sometime on positive side of last sixty years. These things strike out on positive side:

- Self sufficiency in food
- Resurgence in heavy industry
- Quantum leap in information technology
- White Revolution
- Defense strategic equipment

The best monitoring is done by common man as far as a nation is concerned, and I am looking forward to that day, in the near future, when a common man, like the one shown in R.K. Laxmans's cartoon, really rules the country.

***

CHAPTER NINE

Stagnation

Stagnation

One of the major challenges faced by everyone who wants to grow is stagnation. Stagnation is defined as cease to flow, in the dictionary. But in context of growth in human beings and al the enterprises undertaken by human beings it may be that stagnation is multilevel, multi-dimensional term. And it has been used in a very casual way by sales people, by managers and most of all the decision makers.

To me stagnation is the first step towards de-composition or decay. Water, tries to flow, probably "knowing" that standing water is a breeding ground for many undesired germs, which ultimately render it useless. Even the stored water in lakes / dams though looks stationary, has its own way of flowing underground, outside the normal vision of humans.

To prevent stagnation, we should be very dynamic. A birth of a single idea or a concept can create very welcome ripples inside you. Once the action over the idea starts, you are in dynamic phase and for some times have conquered the stagnation. Ideally a person on the move should adopt following preconditions.

1) Talk less - Listen more

2) Eat less - Sleep more

3) Watch less TV - Read more

4) General less - Specific more

5) Reasons less - Results more

- Get new ideas fro every

Possible source.

(1) Talk less listen more – In the primary schools the teacher always told us that the Creator gave us one mouth and two ears, for the simple reason that we should talk less and listen more.

Most of the times in our adult life we tend to forget this and land ourselves in trouble. We tend to forget that words have specific meaning, and utter words we do not mean to. Words can damage relationships in an irreversible manner. You can communicate without words also, and that too very effectively.

A story comes to my mind from some centuries ago. What was said or rather not said, holds good even today,

A story goes like:

Subsequent to their embracing new religion under the guidance of Zorester, the Prophet, the Parsees had a torrid time in Iran, and many of them wanted to flee to India. A ship full of Parsees, landed in Gujarat in the port of Khambayat.

The Parsees were produced in the court and the king was not very interested in the new and unknown influx in his kingdom. It is said that because of the absence of a common language the king produced a glass filled to its brim by milk, so much so that a slight movement caused overflowing. He thought his message was clear and candid.

However, the leader of Parsees was destined to create history. He thought for a while, produced some sugar and added very slowly to glass. After sometime, sugar was permanently mixed with milk without any spillover.

The king was overwhelmed and probably bowled over by this simple gesture and allowed the Parsees to settle down. And since then, the Parsees are the only foreigners on this soil, who have homogeneously, lived with Indian ethos without creating any nuisance.

(2) Eat less sleep more:

To be on the move you should have a control on your diet. Maximum diseases all due to bad food habits, is now accepted by all of us. So do not allow any junk to go inside.

Sleep here is more rest, rather than slumbering. Sleep is a rejuvenation, and if you manage to get up fresh first thing in the morning, you have "well begun" your day.

(3) Watch less TV – Read more:

Television merits a monster status. There have been calculations about many years lost - (Did you say man days? A thing of past, Sir) - due to this more than any other addiction, so far in the entire history of mankind. You know by now that TV is bad, good, useful or useless, in your won way.

Try to develop reading habits which is one thing that shall keep you moving ahead at least on a mental level. Read fiction, non-fiction, newspapers, and periodicals, autobiographies of successful persons, books on a specific topic or without any prejudice, read all that comes your way. You will be more dynamic person within a very short time.

(4) General less specific more:

A generality is a boon to a non-worker. You can go on talking and say nothing if you know how to use generalities. But in the long run these do not help anyone. If you have specific idea a goal, you are more likely to succeed than others. Be specific in what you want, in how many days you want, what method you are adopting to get it, what type of men, machines or tools and amount of money you shall need, and you change into a different person.

(5) Reasons less results more:

This is the ultimate pre-condition for a dynamic person. If you fail, accept your failure first, rather than giving reasons. Reasons have never known to have produced any worthwhile contribution.

(6) Get new ideas from every possible source:

A single idea can change life course of many persons, if properly implemented. Lack of original ideas has been a major source of creating decline of many projects.

Each idea when received should be checked, cross-checked and re-checked again, before its implementation. But a constant flow of new ideas is a vital ingredient in creating a dynamic individual, an organisation or a nation.

To avoid stagnation a simple but golden rule is "Keep working", when you do so you do not have time for:

(a) Speculation - Over one more reason for

your failure in near future or past

(b) Ruminate - Over you mistake and how

you could have made them

or avoided them

(c) You - Stop living in past

(d) You - Work of yourself

(e) You - Try liking what you do

<u>Second line of Management</u>

Stagnation also can be avoided if proper care is taken to create a suitable second line of management. Presently this is best developed by Australian Cricket Team. Their second and third elevens can embarrass many a national team. There has been a intentional effort in doing so, and they are sure of their super status to remain the same way, for years to come.

Ideally, if you are to be promoted you should have nurtured at least two persons to take your position. If you feel threatened in doing so or you feel that you shall be side tracked or in the worst case sacked, then you probably deserve so. Very ruthless, but in other words you have not managed to grow enough, to supervise your own earlier status.

***

CHAPTER TEN

Stoppage of Growth

Stoppage of Growth

Like any other process in life, malfunctioning affects growth also. But because of the casual attitude towards the same, it is diagnosed at a very lat stage. Stoppage of growth is very serious and hence we should look into this perspective very seriously.

Let us find out first the symptoms of this dreaded ailment that affects practically each of us, sometime in course of our life. Some of us realise that something is wrong within us and try to improve; some of us do not realise and pay a very heavy price by way of below par performances, and a poorer quality of life.

I am giving below a list of symptoms on a random basis, found in a person who has stopped growing

(1) - Feeling old

(2) - Shabby appearance

(3) - Lack of appreciation

(4) - Very cynic

(5) - Generally, talks about past glory

(6) - Cries hoarse about his misfortunes

(7) - Unwarranted advices to everyone around him

(8) - General Laud appearance, so as to, attract attention

(9) - Keeps whining about everything

(10) - Self pity

The symptoms may be in various combinations I various persons, and hence may create various degrees of discomfort to the person concerned, but in almost all cases the persons around, suffer very badly, for no fault of theirs.

Let us study each of the above in slightly more details.

(1) Feeling old – The person suffering from this feeling is on the threshold of stoppage of growth. Please note I am saying feeling old. The old person in advanced age is not the one I mean, who is anyway physically old. I mean 'feeling' old, is a person who may be in his thirties or late forties and has already begun saying things like "at my age" etc. Such person is overly worried about his health, and most of his conversation revolves around his lack of energy, enthusiasm or in most cases lack of sleep and its disorders. He is retired, well before his retirement age and keeps on highlighting it. These people have probably never heard that a man is as old as he feels. Their presence in any group is a dampener on the otherwise enthusiastic persons.

Because these persons feel old, display it and hence as a natural response, never volunteer for any new assignment or never offer any initiative. As a result, they are not offered anything worthwhile, which further confirms their thinking "that as they are old, they are side tracked." The time when in all probability, these people are in best position to serve excellently, due to having a rich experience and some "left over' talents, they seal the doors of their own progress.

(2) Shabby appearance – Shabby appearance can be due to very low self esteem, very low opinion about one one's looks, as also due to "for whom to dress up".

Dressing up is primarily for self, and that if it impresses others, is a bonus.

It is prevalent in our country, in cases quite a lot of young ladies, who before their marriage take some care about their dresses, makeup, figure, matching colors, manicure, hair styles, threading, facial massages and so many other things, are suddenly disinterested in their overall appearance, as soon as the first child is born. Probably by then, they feel "secure" and hence tend to neglect the vital aspect of married life, which is a good looking, attractive wife.

Is it any different for the other side of the coin? I do not think so. There is a tremendous scope of improvement. In spite of such an explosion of readymade clothes and various designers, people are still very indifferent about what they wear. They do not realise that one spends approximately same amount of money in wearing shabby clothes as well as clothes which make him / her feel well dressed.

Often an example is quoted about Einstein (torn coat) or the other that of Mahatma Gandhi (his loin cloth) by these shabbily clad people, which is to say the least, is crap. The coat whether torn or not, by itself, is of no value. The <u>value addition</u> comes from the fact that Einstein wore it. The loin cloth was a *constant reminder* to Mahatma, about his mission and poverty of India. It was on purpose he wore what he did. Moreover, why should we concentrate on only the trifles when we can get so many other great things from these two wonderful human beings?

Obesity is another factor; which adds to shabby appearance. To me obesity n most cases is an imbalance between input of food and output of calories burning by way of required exercise. I am simply amazed, when most of the fat people say, that they do not eat much, but still put on weight. How is it possible? Think about it. Best suggestion to these people is to go to a doctor or dietitian and find out for their own surprise, how wrongly they think.

If you yourself are not interested in maintaining your own body and displaying it in a neatly clad fashion, you should sure be on the way of stopped growing.

<u>(3) Lack of appreciation</u> – This is one of the very sure symptoms of people who have stopped growing. They simply cannot say any thing good to anything or any person around them. They may be in direct touch, or not at all concerned with the activity, place, person, they shall never have anything good to say. They will eat, drink, day in day out, as if on a bed in a hospital ward. They will wear a mourning silence, never smile, unless they want to deride someone. These people are probably the most unfortunate lot as they are undergoing a self-inflected torture.

Lack of appreciation is a cover for these people to hide their own insecurity, inferiority complexes. I do not say that all such persons are incompetent or worthless, but what I want say is that they make life difficult for them and for all those people around them. What can be achieved in an easy going, happy way is achieved under a lot of stress and duress.

Lack of appreciation also kills the joy of any worthwhile accomplishment, which is very dangerous. It practically kills any fresh intentions of striving for another achievement or effort to reach new heights. Imagine that you are person working under such a manager, or you are a son of such a father and you will instantly realise what I mean to say.

Like all those things such as smile, sweet talk, clean habits appreciation, also costs nothing, but it improves the quality of life to a great extent. Appreciation of someone else's, smallest achievement can give you biggest joy, which no money can ever buy.

Just think about following situations –

- The first flower to a plant which you have planted in your garden.
- The first smile of your son or daughter.
- The first touch of your beloved.
- The pat on a back by your teacher – and so many other things. You can enjoy and take pleasure from all of this only if you can appreciate. If not, they just pass and the next second onwards, can never be recreated, in spite of the entire wealth of this world.

<u>Very cynic –</u>

Cynic is a person who takes pride in hurting others. Words are like whiplashes, which are used to make others feel small.

I was surprised when I referred to Webster's New Dictionary & Thesaurus and found along with all other meanings "(Greek Kynikos – doglike)" How true?

It was Oscar Wilde who said "Cynic is a person who knows the *price* of everything and *value* of nothing."

In most cases cynics are very intelligent and if they wish they can serve the humanity in a very distinguished way but they choose to vilify, to hurt, to cut to size, all people who are unfortunate to be in the vicinity. Why do they do it? God knows?

They enjoy failures of everyone around them and rhetorically say "I knew it".

<u>Generally, talks about past / past glory</u>

You must be having a lot of such persons in your circle. They talk mostly of the past. What they do not realise is they talk of pat and its glory, because they do not have anything worthwhile in the present. Because present is blank or black, the future is not to be even thought of.

To all such people the past is hammock, rather than a spring board, lying there, they keep on saying all things they would be better off not saying.

If Tendulkar is batting, they will always talk of Gavaskar without realizing that the two concerned (Tendulkar / Gavaskar) are very good to each other. (As it is when you are in first playing eleven playing in any era, out of 100 crores, your have to be exceptionally good.) Nostalgia can be good provided it gives you some base fro which you can step forward.

<u>Cries hoarse about his misfortunes-</u>

If you believe in what such a person has to say about him and his fortunes you should feel that mankind ha been put to an irreversible loss. This man so good, could have done so much, but for his misfortunes, that too, on a continuous basis. So engrossed these people in their misfortunes that they do not prepare themselves to grab whatever little "less" misfortunes they come across.

They, do not have any inkling about 'luck' can be more or less produced, by – adding a "p" – pluck. The intensity, with which they keep on cursing their luck, needs a little reorientation to put their life in a proper perspective.

<u>Unwarranted advices to everyone around them</u>.

Whether it is needed, or not, whether it is asked or not, whether it is welcome or not, these people keep on bombarding advices, suggestions to everyone around them. They will advise a doctor on a surgery, a lawyer on his argument, Sachin, on his square cut, and so on and so forth. In the "terminal" cases of this ailment it becomes so bad, that other people start running away as soon as "these people" are within sight.

Advice comes free and hence dispensed without any mercy.

General loud appearance so as to attack attention: -

Because of a vary low self esteem, coupled with inability to do anything worthwhile, such people are facing a constant aversion form their friends (if any still left), colleagues (unfortunate lot), spouse and children (what can we say about them). It hurts to a great extent, but because such people can not comprehend the correct reasons for the treatment meted out to them, try turning 'loud' which further aggravates the problem. Earlier they had their problems, created some discomfort to others, but now due to their loudness, they are turned into a distinct nuisance.

To attract attention they talk loudly, pick up arguments, laugh unnaturally, flirt with opposite sex, in some chronic cases even feign illness. In doing so, they defeat the basic purpose of their action. They may get a permanent ridicule and aversion.

They dress in absolutely shocking colors, use very strong perfumes, and live in their own world of imagination, where is they are the "centre of attraction".

The difference between these two worlds, the one they imaging and the one they actually are forced to live in, causes a great stress which ultimately creates an irreversible damage. The more they want to bridge this gap, the more it widens ultimately, forcing the person to submit meekly to his unfortunate lot.

Keeps whining about everything

These people are an unfortunate lot. They simply cannot enjoy even the basic things in life. They always want, what is presently not available. On a bright sunny day, they shall bitterly complain about heat, without even realizing that sunshine is to be enjoyed. On a rainy day they shall complain about humidity, and winter always produces body ache, cold and cough etc.

To be unable to find anything good, in every activity in your life requires special genetic combination. Nothing is good for these people and hence they are not good for anyone. They can kill any happy ambience absolutely effortlessly.

They have an inbuilt resistance to anything new, which may improve their own lots. Lack of initiative, lack of capacity to listen to other persons leads to the to the foregone conclusion, which is stoppage of growth.

Self-Pity –

A senior doctor who has seen practically all sides of human form and habits once told me "Self pity is the worst ailment a person can suffer from. It s worse than Cancer, Ulcer, Tumor, Diabetes and any other disease you may think of." Such a statement needed explanation and he further said in his own style, "All other diseases can be cured, can be fought with, can be managed and monitored but in case of self pity there is only one end".

When inflected with self pity, the basic desire to fight, itself goes away, creating all problems. They are so convinced about their misfortunes that they cannot even imagine that something good can happen to them.

As it is when a person takes pity on some one else, it is understood, that the someone else, is a "lower form" of life, needs some free help. This help generally called as alms, charity, can help "the someone else" to survive, but in no case can imbibe a feeling of self respect. Once used to taking free help; the slide begins very fast to the end.

And when the person taking pity is "you", and "some one else" is also "you", can you imagine the resultant bitterness? Self pity also means that you do not like yourself, which is a big irony and is totally against the spirit of the very existence of human life.

This level of disidentification is very detrimental and unless properly dealt with by way of proper counseling or encouragement from those who matter, can be a total disaster for the person indulging in self pity.

A person suffering from self-pity takes failures for granted and also, he has an exaggerated notion, about his problems.

The symptoms displayed in the person, who have stopped growing are so conspicuously visible and cause such a great discomfort, that even though on knows that it should be treated like a disease, cannot do so. Even if one wants to sympathies with such a lot, cannot bring himself to do so. General aversion, neglect and ridicule are the responses fro the society towards such people, which further confirms that these people may not be brought back to normal run of life.

<u>Reasons for stoppage of growth:</u>

What are the **reasons** for such a downfall? Why cannot a person live a normal human life expected to give happiness and in some cases fulfillment? Are there reasons, if present, can they be avoided?

There are many **reasons** which have been found out, researched on, but the principal reasons can be at random cited as:

1. Monotony
2. Security of job
3. Jealousy
4. Resistance to changes
5. Nagging spouse
6. Bad health
7. Level of incompetence

Let us deal with one by one

(1) <u>Monotony</u> – Doing something again and again, over a long period of time sets in monotony, which is one of the biggest reasons for stoppage of growth. Human intelligence is divided into two categories; such as Basis and Specific.

<u>Basic Intelligence</u> – Which is more desirable as it can be used to apply for learning new things, which avoids monotony. These people are more creative, more analytical and can generally adapt to any given situation in life.

<u>Specific Intelligence</u> is what you acquire by doing repetitive things for example, a clerk in government office shall have achieved specific intelligence required to do his job. He knows inside out of the procedure and can be treated as an expert. But a minor deviation here and there and he is very uncomfortable. The security of procedures, when violated makes him very vulnerable to fits of anger, desperation. Most of the human population fall in the second category, which in itself is a reason fro

stoppage of growth.

The person belonging to both the above categories respond differently to the monotonous situation and hence achieve different results, the person with basic intelligence strives to find out how they can better their performance, they strive to learn something new and in such an effort, get promoted and avoid monotony. Not so in the case the persons in the second category.

I would love to narrate a story, which may explain my point of view.

The story pertains to Indian Railways which in itself is almost a miracle. How it works producing results, day in day out, is always a matter of fascination to me.

Any way, in our story, Ramji was to retire from railways after putting in 33 years of service. He was working in maintenance department and his job was to strike a hammer on the wheels, when ever the train arrived on a platform.

The day of his retirement coincided, with the conclusion of "service with a smile" week and the DRM (Divisional Railway Manger) thought it would be good for the moral of the staff, if he also graced the farewell ceremony. Accordingly, everything was going as per plan. All people were happy, Ramaji was happy until this happened.

The DRM called Ramji on the stage – saying that no matter how insignificant any job might be, it formed a vital part in the smooth operation of Indian Railways.

The DRM asked "Ha! Ramji what was your job?"

Ramji – "Huzur! Striking a hammer on the wheels".

DRM – "How many years did you do it?"

Ramji – "33 years! Huzur!"

DRM – "Why did you do it? Do you know the reason?"

Ramji – "Ha! Huzur! My father did it before me, that's why".

The function was <u>over</u> that instant, The DRM did not know where to look.

Ramji, for 33 yeas hammered the railway wheels without knowing "why".

How many persons you know around you who resemble Ramji? What sort of growth can happen to such people?

Why can't any measures be taken to avoid the monotony?

(2) <u>Security of Job</u>:

It has been seen that a person when on probation works with more interest, more commitment. As soon as the person it confirmed (especially in govt. dept.) something drastically changes, within his mental framework, which makes him feel, more relaxed, in the initial stages and callously negligent in the latter stages. This results in the low quality of work causing a loss on an irreversible scale in the growth of our nation.

The leaders especially from trade unions, also add to the problems. These leaders have been talking of labor rights, without ever mentioning their duties and responsibilities. Where are these labor leaders, when the "capitalist" entrepreneur in working overtime to set up his unit? Where are they when the unit is struggling to find its feet, in the fiercely competitive world? As soon as the unit becomes profitable all the labor leaders rush in for their share of pound of flesh. If all enterprises were to close down, how many leaders would continue to exist? If the host dies how many parasites can survive? But the person is told that it is because of him the industry runs, which is falsification. No number of workers and leaders can start from a scratch an industry, as it takes much more them mere union of people.

The security of a job tends to create more passengers rather than active participants, in the process of creating money. The knowledge that it is not necessary to improve, can lead to stoppage of growth.

(3) <u>Jealousy</u> – Jealousy works both ways. It can spur the growth response in some, while in others it can deactivate the basic desire to grow. For those, who think that success is a function of luck, jealousy tends to paralyze their thinking and activity. They instead of working on their goals, waste their time in finding out how the other person, (ever so lucky) got the success without deserving.

(4<u>) Resistance to changes</u> – Any change, in any present procedure, has an inherent potential to affect the procedure. If properly understood and handled, then the changes can create positive impulse. The problem starts when the changes as a whole are opposed. To grow you have to have a dynamic view of your life. If you have to change the way you live it is obligatory on you to change the way you think.

Agreed that all changes cannot be good bud it is also obvious that unless you accept to change nothing changes.

Somethings in life never change, whereas some other things always change. Somethings in life should never change where as some other things is life have to change.

Life is always considered on a dynamic scale and hence I shall try to explain "changes" by taking a very common example of a busy sub-urban square where 2 roads cross each other.

(a) At any given instant of time the traffic of these roads is an example of dynamic changes. If you take a movie, frame by frame the situation is never the same. Somethings have changed.

(b) At the same time there are somethings which have not changed. The roads are same, the lights are same, the street signs are same yet it appears that everything keeps on changing.

(c) Most importantly unless you are a part of this dynamic phase system, it really does not matter to you. If you are on this road, then a red light, a rash driver, someone over speeding, a rare failure of brakes, a beautiful companion with you, somebody saving a small kid, somebody escorting a visually handicapped person to the other side of road, a buffalo squatting right in the middle nonchalantly ruminating, should be a part of an experience to you, or otherwise you may choose to be at your home and are out of the picture.

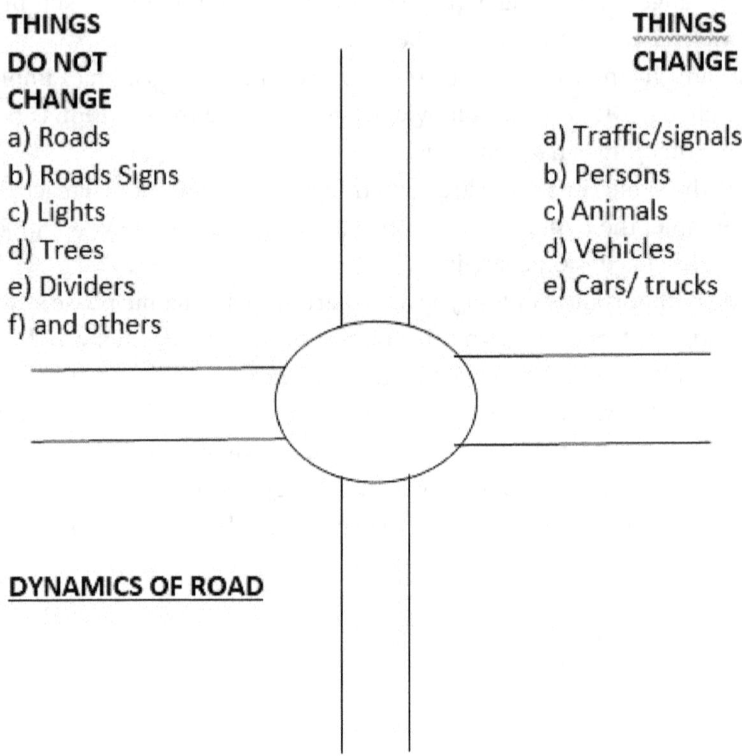

Dynamics of Road

(d) You and your interactions with the changes occurring in the world around you also can be explained in the same way. If you choose to be a part of the changes happening around you, it is good for you. **With you or without you the world will run** its own way, the fun lies in **trying to change** it to suit our own way.

People who are deemed to have stopped growing resist change, even without listening or paying any attention to what the change might do to them. To them any change means readjustments, accommodation and hence painful.

(5) Nagging spouse

To a common man, one of the biggest factors which resist his growth or in some cases totally, puts a halt to the growth is the "spouse". It does not matter whether it is a man or a woman, as both of them have equal potential of nuisance value, as far as stopping of growth is concerned. Psychotherapists have put marriage as one of the most important factors, which changes life, second only t death. A nagging wife / partner can be a major factor in stoppage of growth.

This statement cuts both ways. The classical statement that behind every successful man there is a woman needs to be seen n a different perspective. As my psychotherapist friend says "It is only when the man is successful, the wife steps in".

Because of the very nature of this complex relationship of married life, each partner is in a position to cut the other to his or her size. To rise above the normal level, it takes a person of the stature of Socrates (Xantippe) or more recently our own Sant Tukaram. In one of his poetic creations (called Abhang – which cannot break) Tukaram Maharaj, actually thanks his Vitthala (incarnation of Shri Krishna) for the extreme nagging nature of his wife – Jijabai. The saint says that because of her constant nagging only, he could find solace in devotion. Nothing else could have offset her nagging.

To us more common people if we have to grow, we have to have our own individual each couple specific adjustment lever. The ones who have it, and move importantly are using it have better chances of surviving and hence growing.

(6) Bad Health

Many careers have been ruined due to untimely health hazards. Industries, kingdoms have suffered because of bad health of the persons who mattered.

Shivaji Maharaj died at a wrong time, when he was around fifty years old. Sambhaji was just thirty when he was tortured to death by Aurangzeb. Bajirao Peshwa, the first, died at the age of 32, where a Madhav Rao Peshwa (senior) died when he was only 26. I am sure the history would have been different but for the bad health of these great Maratha leaders. The vacuum created by the untimely deaths could never be properly filled in, ultimately resulting in an abrupt end of what could have been a continued glorious chapter in Indian History.

You can find so many such examples where in a temporary fall in health of a person who matters, causing a near permanent setback in the growth of an enterprise. So along with all other responsibilities, the growth-oriented person has to look with his own health. He must find time to keep himself fit, if not fighting fit. the time invested by him to keep him fit can turn out to be the most profitable one, in the end.

<u>(7) Setting in of level of incompetence</u>

Level of incompetence, is a fairly recent concept, which is extremely interesting, and can explain quite a few things about capacity and ability of a person, and his subsequent accomplishment, in a very fascinating way.

The Peter Principle, was first introduced by Lawrence J. Peter in the book with the same title. The book deals with the downfalls of the bureaucratic organisations.

The book says that in any hierarchically structured organisation, people tend to get promoted up to their level of incompetence. In a course of ideal situation people get employed at a relatively lower level or ranks, get competent enough to perform the job and as a reward, get promoted. To a higher-ranking position, which, naturally requires higher level of ability and competence. Though this seems very logical and hence should continue on an indefinite scale. It does not. The process is disturbed by the people who though get promoted; find that they are no longer competent enough to discharge proper function, required at the next level. Most of the times people do not "wish" to be promoted even though they may not accept this fact. They may be in fact happier and willing to work at a lower level.

But since the working conditions, the contracts, work towards promoting a person predominantly on a time bound parameter rather than competence, may result into senior positions occupied by incompetent persons. This is very disturbing situation and it can also mean that most of the senior positions are not having a right person. It also means that we irrespective of our present-day levels, we are destined to reach our levels of incompetence in the future.

Level of incompetence can be categorised into 4 stages which may occur singularly or in an overlapping way.

(1) Unconsciously incompetent:

The employees falling in this category **do not know** that they **do not know** how to accomplish a certain task or goal.

(2) Consciously incompetent - Here the employees know **that "they do not know".**

(3) Consciously competent –

The employees in this class know that "they know how to perform, (them is they know that they are competent) but to actually deliver they have to work with a lot of focus and continuous effort.

(4) Unconsciously competent -

The employees in this category are basically "doers". They do the things without the proverbial "thinking".

Please note that when this concept of "level of incompetence" was launched, it created much more than a ripple. All junior levels and middle levels employees gleefully accepted and went gaga over it, without realizing, they were very soon to be next in the chopping line. Even today the senior bureaucrats do not respond to this concept for every obvious reason.

I feel that this concept though very interesting, has its own shortcomings. It punctures the balloon of accomplishments of people who go up. It undermines the strength of training activity as a whole. It also creates a feeling of a helplessness for the organizational experts, because according to this concept whatever they do, the end result will be that the senior positions at any given time are to be occupied by persons who are at their respective levels of incompetence.

Interestingly, if applied in Indian conditions it overlooks one major category of "Intentionally Incompetent". The people of this category are to be found in plenty in public sector rather than private sector. Based on a very lopsided concept, "You cannot make mistakes, if you do not work, because you do not make mistakes, you get promoted." This is a situation which should be avoided at all costs.

Is there any solution to this?

Scott Adams, the creator of Dilbert, a cartoon strip, widely published in American Print Media, thought about this.

He in an article in The Wall Street Journal of May 22, 1995 formulated "The Dilbert Principle", which says that most ineffective workers are systematically moved to a position, where they can cause the least damage.

But what about the damage that has already been affected? What about the cascading effects of the damages due to wrong decisions taken by the "incompetent" decision makers, before they were shunted to positions where they were considered safe, within acceptable limits of tolerance? What about the opportunity costs, because of the lost opportunities? What about the cost of stopped growth?

Let us apply this in Indian Scenario, Prithiviraj Chouhan, who had forgiven Mohammad Ghori for 16 times reportedly and once only when Ghori defeated him, he killed Chouhan. This unnecessary gesture opened the floodgates for future invasions by the Mughals. A wrong decision regarding Jammu and Kashmir in 1947. What is the cost in terms of money, loss of life, which could have been otherwise used in a more productive way, an avoidable loss of invaluable human lives, the expense of three wars, and now a proxy war? Can you actually calculate the costs?

The decision to reorganize the states on language basis, the decision to nationalize the banks, the coal fields, the steel plants, the power sector, the railways, the decision on reservations and its continuation, all need an honest review and audit.

In my time, itself, I have seen a big turn around over nationalization and privatization. In 1970's everything that was private was bad, hence nationalized. In 2000 the reversal occurred. I think the decision makers have a missed the point altogether. The point of common denominator, whether a public sector or a private sector, both have to work with Indian people. Unless some drastic steps are taken to improve the work culture / ethics of all of us, Indians, the pendulum from public to private to public will keep on swinging, and may achieve practically nothing, except huge losses.

Indian people and India as a whole have a is going up tremendous resilience. Can you name of country where the GDP in increasing in spite of billions of rupees lost to revenue, through stock exchange scam, telephone scam, fodder scam, the Telgi Revenue Stamp scam, the 2G/ 3G scams, the ever-present parallel economy and many other scams which are yet to be unmasked. I think you may get my point of view.

The strongest asset and liability in India is the same. The population. The day when even half of Indians start taking interest is the welfare of their nation, nobody can stop India to emerge as the best country in the world to live in.

Even today we are good but we can be better if we learn to

- be more conscientious.
- be more honest
- put country before an individual
- stop hero worship
- develop integrity
- work towards developing the national image
- put an end to religious, communal outrages
- be intolerant to corrupt people.

***

CHAPTER ELEVEN

Scope of Growth

Scope of Growth

It is very interesting to think on these lines. If we know what growth is all about, then we should also understand that growth is an unending process, in an ideal situation. But during the course or journey towards one or the other objective, man tries to rationalize which results in the limiting of growth. The beauty of the process lies in the fact that whatever has been achieved today, was considered to be impossible, and what is highly improbable today, shall be achieved in the future.

Because growth is to be seen on a holistic basis, and to be understood with all the variables involved, a question should be always addressed to: how far one can go in the pursuit of this unending process? The answer should be infinity, because once you achieve a goal, the next logical goal should automatically prop up in your mind.

On a practical scale, let us see what can be done with reference to some of the common professions. The professions we interact with, in our day-to-day routine. Logical conclusions on the basis of what we know today can be interesting. These conclusions by themselves if achieved can be wonderful achievements, but they should to open doors to their next levels.

Education

Any student when admitted to pre-primary class can rise to very high levels. It is possible, but highly improbable, which makes it very interesting.

From

KG-I

SSC

Graduation - B.Sc., B.A., B.Com.,

B.E., M.B.B.S.

Post Graduation - M.Sc., M.A., M.Com.,

M.E., Ms / MD

Ph.D. - Ph.D
To
Post Doctoral - D.Sc.
Qualifications

Let us assume that <u>one person out of say one million</u> has achieved a D.Sc. Does it mean that he has grown to maximum? I think, yes and no. He has a D.Sc. but it is related to fraction of knowledge available to him. He has limited his scope, got specialized proficiency, but he should himself know that, there is much more to be learnt.

Probably it was Socrates who said centuries ago that a person, who knows most, knows that, he knows nothing. Acquiring knowledge is really very relative. What we know about our own planet is rudimentary in terms of absolute. We have achieved a lot, we should be proud for our achievements, but we should never ever forget that we may have just scratched the tip of the proverbial iceberg. We still do not know so many things. Do we really know about the centre of the earth? Do we have any idea about exact situation at the bottom of the oceans? Do we really know about space, galaxies? What about AIDS Corona or Cancer? And please remember that all these questions are still unanswered, even when attempted by the cumulative intelligence of the entire mankind. Actually, the scenario becomes even more complex when we think that probably, we do not know what we yet do not know.

Do you now realise that extent of educational growth possible, may be in centuries to come? The pride of what we know, the pride of knowledge which people put on display, suddenly appears very childish.

<u>**Sports:**</u>

Sports is a huge activity, which includes so many games, events, individual participation, teams working to win, at various levels, at which sports are played, shapes sizes of the playing arena, and so on and so forth. The sheer extent of diversity is too big to comprehend.

In the most popular game of cricket, a bowler can get a wicket with every ball he bowls, a batsman can score a sic, off every ball he faces. Very improbable, but can not be ruled out as totally impossible. Sometime in the future this feat shall also be achieved. The limits are yet to be achieved in any game, but once achieved, they seem to be more than often repeated. In classic case of "4 minutes for a mile", now it seems normal, though not at all easy by any standards.

In the single player games, such as running, swimming, tennis, badminton, the sportsman is fighting his opponent for a particular event, but many times more, he is fighting with his inner self for achieving the present day "impossible." However, as he grows in stature, there is always much more left to be won. This feeling of "what nest" is the constant motivating factor for all those who want to break present day records.

<u>Science and technology:</u>

It constitutes a glorious chapter in the human existence. We have achieved so much in so many fields, yet we have no knowledge, even on a rudimentary level, when many other fields are considered. Even today the best pump still remains the human heart, the best filter – the kidneys. The minimal requirement of resources to deliver the almost miraculous results is yet to be fully understood by us, leave aside their creation, artificially.

When it was decided to put man on the moon, there were many problems to be resolved. One such problem was a pen which could defy the gravity. It is said that the U.S. scientists developed such a pen at a cost of one million dollars. On the other side Russians simply used a pencil. The above may be a story, but it gives a clear message. Do not get away from practically available solutions. When we consider the earth as a part of a galaxy, we know how small we are, further we know that our galaxy it self, is a fraction of other galaxies, then we many try to get our picture in a proper perspective. On this backdrop, the fights of terrorists, one country fighting another, are reduced to a ridiculous level.

Our forefathers were smart; they knew the value of self and self-enlightenment. They could probably use the powers of light, sound, fire, water and space in a much simpler and better way, than us. They also knew the value of such knowledge; hence they did not leave any easy clues for its access to us.

The more we think we know the more ridiculous we may appear in the absolute context. The super intelligence in one field actually should open doors to many other fields, where we have to once again start from a scratch. As far as today, it we know, what we do not know, should be enough for us to launch in the pursuit of such excellence, to be found in unknown mazes of darkness (again assumed) so as to reach the goal of ultimate enlightenment. The second stage of this journey is we should know that we do not know what we should know, and how to acquire such knowledge. The scope of growth hence is quite incomprehensible as we do not as yet perceive growth in its true form and potential.

The potential is a term which needs a constant reminder to achieve its full value. The human potential is a subject which is discussed by the intellectuals for centuries. Why a man with immense talents is not where he should be and how a person branded as a mere mediocre is able to reach dizzy heights, unimaginable for the most. What is the real answer to this? The early promises and estimates sometimes match with the performances of a person in the future, but in most cases, it is a matter of what could have been rather than what it is, as on today.

Skip Ross, the legendary trainer and motivational speaker says that the man should always ask himself: 'Is he where he was created to be'? It seems very simple, but to pinpoint the accurate level is extremely difficult even for a person allowed a free hand for wishful thinking. No strings attached, what is the maximum one can think about himself and his position in the future can turn out as the maximum he can reach and extract from one life.

I always have said and I confirm once more that I have yet to see a negative child. The child is happy, all positive image of human being. Something down the line starts going awry and in most cases by the time he is 'accepted' as a mature adult he has usually a very low view of himself and the society. If we are able to find an answer to this, may be, we would hope for a proper matching of desired and achieved levels of human excellence.

When a person condemned to be a failure, finally achieves something beyond the imagination of the ones who out rightly had earlier condemned him is like a case of eating the proverbial hat. Not to be outdone, the smart ones claim that the achiever was just plain lucky. How great? A handicapped person achieving great feats is not uncommon, a Milton, a Beethoven, a Sudha Chandran, a Surdas, a Stephan Hawking are the examples which amply state that the people with indomitable spirit realize their potential which out shines the achievements of so many so-called complete people. The para-Olympics glorifies the indomitable human spirit. A son of a Sanyasi, persecuted and humiliated beyond limits, writes an epic which is a topic of PhD's, even after 800 years. History is full of such lessons and yet every time an unlikely person needs some understanding the world offers him a cold shoulder. Potential is not a monopoly of any class, creed or color, but it is not accepted as it is. In our religion it is said (very rarely accepted) if a man wills, he can turn himself in God. (*Nar agar karni kare to nar se narayan ban jaye*). I feel, the ultimate peak of human potential is to be the Creator Himself and each of us has been blessed with the potential to be the one. Some time in our life we had it or some one even today has it, to what effect we are putting it to use is for every one to see.

So, the question is not whether one has the potential, it is always there. The question is what he does with it? Too many people with immense potential have lived their lives wandering aimlessly. Each day, such people awaken to a new day, but crib about the same unsolved problems, pending and unresolved for months, even years and ages before. Unused potential even today remains the single largest problem of human existence.

The promise of a potential and the subsequent performance generally have a lot of grey areas, which are posing a big challenge. A person with potential is not mostly aware of his strengths, here some one may be a teacher, trainer, a god father or any other well wisher has to play a major role by not only reminding the person but more importantly initiate the process. One has to realize that the initial resistance is due to the inertia and lack of preparations. The mentor can roll the ball which subsequently gathers its own momentum and becomes self sustaining and supporting system.

The promised potential rolls in to a performing phase, which is watched by the world like a hawk. A mistake here, a short fall there is highlighted. It is a saddening experience and may result in the abrupt end of the process. The performer has to adopt a philosophical attitude and should be able to actually thank such fault finders as they are inadvertently helping to improve the system and the process in the end.

The appraisal of the used and unused potential has been a concern. How can one be sure that a person has put in a complete effort and yet the results are not matching? Do we have time to really review the entire process? The usual appraisal process is very different for self and others. The performance should be such that who appraises it should not matter, as they say number one is generally number one.

The distance between the promise and the performance has a major bridge, which has two vital piers, namely persistence and perseverance. In the end it is usually the ones who succeed are those who run slightly longer, some how manage the stress slightly better. The little difference is the deciding factor between the promise and fulfillment of the potential.

The scope of the growth is to estimate, understand and achieve the potential of ourselves. Some body has to tell us:

"You are the best; DO YOU KNOW IT?"

***

CHAPTER TWELVE

Corruption

Corruption

Once of the major issues facing most of the nations, at the various developmental stages is corruption. Unfortunately, this phenomenon is present in the poorer countries in a very high scale. Money blocked in corruption is the major reason for the stopping of growth. The bribes are given to cover up the irregularity, which means that the below standard quality of the works executed, is accepted. The goods of below par of accepted norms are accepted creating a parallel economy. The result of corruption is hampered development and hence one who wants to grow should think about corruption as a major evil and fight it using all his resources. Everybody in the organisation is aware about corruption talks freely about it. But when tackled for the stopping of corruption, he just either pleads helplessness or smiles cynically at you questioning the very sanity of such a question.

The problem-solving techniques tell us that the most important step, towards finding the solution to any problem is to correctly identify the problem, itself. In case of corruption, we know what our problem is. Asking questions about anything is to the questions asked. I have been asking quite a few questions about corruption as a whole, and with a special interest in our country. I am trying to put forward my answers to the questions asked by me. I would really love to see India, at the top of world in all the activities which should make us a proud nation.

It is up to you to either accept, then modify or just reject it on an outright basis. But importantly you should start to think.

In his book, "We the people". Nani Palkhiwala has discussed this aspect very candidly. In fact, everybody should read this book, especially the part, where Mr. Palkhiwala compares the Indians with the Japanese.

Corruption, in our country as on today is an accepted phenomenon. It almost has a gazetted status. The state of affairs is quite mind-boggling. We have stated singing praises of even those officers who are corrupt, but do their job, as there are many others who accept bribes, but fail to do the promised job. Very disgusting to say the least!

Corruption to me is a personal decision and apart from a personal weakness there can be no justification, if you may call it so, for corruption. Whatever may be the compulsions, you may still be honest, if you desire to be. Any other reason, which can be one of the many standard reasons – such as political pressures, transfers, need of money, inter personal relationships, pressure from the superiors, can be a whitewash.

It is also said that as long as, there is one who wants to give and the other who wants to take, it shall be very difficult to curb this corruption menace. It is also debated very passionately as to where the corruption menace. It is also debated very passionately as to where the corruption starts, it the lower cadres or in the high places. It is also stated with a plain face that what one man can do, when the system is itself corrupt. All this, is again a very convenient way of trying to justify your wrongs. On an absolute level you know whether you are corrupt, willingly or unwillingly. You may give reasons for your weakness, but it only confirms that you are corrupt. People have a fascinating way of setting their own standards. Businessmen, go out of their way to explain how high rates of taxation, corrupt officialdom, compel them to do what they, reluctantly have to do. Search of ideal conditions is a wild goose chase. It is guaranteed that such conditions shall never prevail.

One should try to analyse to spending of such money generated because of corruption. Is it spent on anything worthwhile? Does it make you feel good? The only places such money goes are the ones where you would not allow your wife or your daughter to step in.

So again, corruption is an issue, that is personal to begin with, becomes too large when it is seen on a social level, and becomes absolutely incomprehensible when viewed on a national or an international level.

Can we really fight corruption? The answer lies in whether we want to? May be the concept of "Self-Deception" should throw some light on the interaction between a normal citizen and an ever-present corruption. The book "Leadership and Self-Deception" has a very interesting concept which should be analyzed by each person on his own level. To put the concept in simple language, it is said that a person knows what he should rightly do, somehow does not do, and then keeps on finding reasons for his inaction. The process of finding such reasons is an act of "Self-Deception." Every common man with a normal set of values knows that corruption is evil and he should not indulge in any of such corrupt practices, but he does not listen to his inner voice, and then keeps on finding reasons. The reasons, which he thinks would give him a false sense of self esteem and also some justification if he can call it so.

The question, each one of us has to answer, is "Can I say NO"? Take a common case of a TTE (Traveling Ticket Examiner) and passengers in a train. Why the TTE is able to make money? If no passenger wants to pay "extra" for the berth he is not rightfully entitled to, can the TTE still make money? We know that we are wrong in paying extra, but we do pay, and then try to find reasons for our incorrect behavior. The extent of such a "small" deal, calculated on a single train basis, and then projected on a scale of entire operations of Indian Railways, may reach something like Rs. 3 to 4 million, per day basis. The same logic applied on railway goods traffic, catering services, retiring rooms, material handling, purchases required for railways, irregularities of the computer booking of railway tickets, contracts, involving construction and maintenance, and all such activities, where money is involved, can give you a "figure" which you will find absolutely mind-boggling. But remember one simple thing. It all began with you or someone like you who could have said "No!".

Let us turn our attention to what should be done, by all of us Indians, to fight corruption and *at least theoretically* have a **Corruption Free India**. Even though, your rational, reality oriented and practical set of minds tell you that it is not possible, please think about it. Think about the possible rewards to you and your family, if such a condition is achieved in, may be even 10 years from today. So run down your laconic smile and cynical attitude, and get ready to live in a corruption free India.

(1) The first requirement toward such a nation is to have a generation of students, who believe in themselves. Students who believe in fair competition; who get angry over wrong things and are fiercely patriotic.

If you are asked to go back to your school days, you should remember that you were generally a happy child, with very high belief levels, in everything that was good. As you graduated, something went wrong and you joined the "practical" band of Indians. The impressions which were supposed to last for the lifetime, could not survive the pressure, resulting in present day 'you'.

We have to devise methods which will highlight the significance of morals and ethics. The intentional emphasis on the correct behavior should be to create a solid moral and ethical foundation, in the minds of young students which should last a lifetime. These things work and have been working, but on a lesser scale. The moral education is the biggest single factor which allows a human being to stay on a course.

Every Indian school book has a first page saying "India is my country; All Indians are my brother" etc. The massage is very correct and if all students really believe of then we may not have any tensions as regards community, religions etc. But probably the method in which the message is given to the students can be better. The teacher who teaches this message should be more enthusiastic. The tone many times is almost very near to ridicule and hence the parroting of the message can be very comical. Seriously, if the teachers do not believe what they teach, they should be some where else rather than teaching.

The parents, who pay the fees to the school and to private tuitions, tend to conveniently forget **that parenting is a full-time job.** Their children are primarily their responsibility and not of the teachers. Both teachers and parents have to remember one thing very clearly that the children may or may not listen to what they (teachers and parents) say, but the children certainly see and copy what their parents or teachers do. One wrong lesson learnt by the children, would have a cascading effect, on the children, society and finally on the ethical fabric of the nation. A teacher or a parent tends to forget that he is a role model for his children, which affects the seriousness of the education imparted by both of them. Both, the parents or the teachers have no time for the children, but somehow find time to put the blame on each other.

Correct moral / ethical education shall be the first step towards a corruption free India.

(2) The second step to ensure is to have a free flow of correct information. The right to information is nestled in the constitution books only. If has to come out in open. Every Indian who seeks to have any information should be taught how to find it, where to find it, how to use it. Electronic media print media have been instrumental in this direction but in a lopsided way. Their flow of information is not without bias. Especially, English news media has to improve a lot. There is hardly any positive input in the information doled out on 24 hours basis. Highlighting, trifle issues, lousy antics of "Netas", downgrading of Hinduism, should be avoided.

Channels in English keep on harping about the wrongs in Hindu religion. That, they cannot find anything wrong in any other religion or community is an enigma itself and the same reflects in their programs. The perverse picture presented is not what Hinduism is all about. Probably it is the tolerant attitude of Hindus, which allows these channels to dish out the trash, they do. It is very fashionable for these channels to equate Hinduism, and Hindu community with backwardness, or fundamentalism, which is not true. Probably they lack guts to do an impartial analysis. Any person with rudimentary knowledge of Hindu religion and history of India, shall be able to analyse the pseudo-intellectual analysis given by such anchors and their programmers

The computerization and information explosion through wireless communication methods, have already shown some exciting results in the last decade or so, sooner the common Indian realizes the power of information and its subsequent potential to create resources, the better it shall be for India. Let the common Indian get the information, analyse it (contrary to publicized belief) and use it, for his own good.

(3) Let profit be the keyword!

Profit is a dirty word as far as socialists were concerned. I was always very amused, when practically on Indian businessman, in the early seventies could openly talk about profits. They talked about social duties of business houses, equality of opportunity, but probably none believed in it.

Business is done for the profit. Let us reiterate this sentence. We have seen, the mess created by confusing goals of social reform and business. A business is primarily done for profit, and anything else it may achieve, is a bonus.

As a country on a move the private enterprise must be encouraged. After all, elsewhere in the world they have ben successful beyond any doubt. The privatization, properly handled can be a major key to a corruption free India. I do not subscribe to the view of extremes that anything in private sector is the best and vice versa. The mixed model of economy though sounds very good to listen to, has outlived its life. The job security, without any attached responsibility should be viewed with contempt.

Whether the unit is in public or private sector the keyword should be profit. All thriving and profit-making units, shall boost the economy, creating the "real' money, which may put an end to number 2 or 3 types of money. By profit I mean real profit, not the type which was prevalent before the "non performing assets" concept in the banking sector.

(4) Justice procedures: Justice delayed in justice denied has lost all impact in the judicial system in India. Probably one of the biggest breeding grounds of corruption is the judiciary itself. Why it has stooped to such a low level is known to every Indian, but because it can not be proved in the court, it still continues to operate in the same fashion. When formal judiciary was formed by the Britishers in India, their purpose was not to give justice to the public, but to help their Raj, to rule and exploit. The delays as and when suited to them, or the quick disposal of cases, when it was needed was the basis of the British Judicial system in India, in British Raj. I for one can never believe that the British were fair to anybody except themselves. How could they be?

But, what about us, the Indians? Are we fair to our people? Why the judicial courts have so many holidays, vacations when more than crores of cases pending in the various courts? Under the garb of some outdated logic the cases are kept running for years and generations. Can a normal case be over and ready for judgment, within say 7 hearings? Can we have a system where the judge can decide, whether or not eh case should be admitted for further hearing or needs a dismissal? Can there be any control over the casual allotment of dates? Can there be a time limit of say 6 months for the case from its admittance to the final hearing? I think all the intelligent, learned, patriotic judicial authorities should at least, once take the initiative and do something which should ensure speedy and correct justice, to us the common Indians. Instead of the usual "holier than thou" attitude and the "scoff", the people who matter should initiate measures, before it is too late.

(5) Election Reforms

Every time this term is used; it starts a debate which leads to nothing, but a further debate. I have been listening to this type of debates since last about six decades; with no conclusion.

To expect that such reforms shall take place in a natural course is a myth. Why would anyone kill, a golden egg laying hen? The gang leaders who are supposed to loot and plunder in elections and subsequent to the results, are never interested in any reforms.

When T.N. Seshan was asked about how could, his answer was very simple and sincere. He said that he followed the rules, already present in election manuals. As soon as he retired, the negative effect was once again visible. The key to reforms lies probably not in rules but in the implementation of the rules. The biggest comedy is on when the elections in India are on.

If in spite of all rules and regulations, we get the "people" we are forced to elect then something is seriously wrong in our electoral process. In fact, whenever a debate on leadership is initiated, we have to sadly exclude, the political leadership, in India. This is one of the worst developments in the recent decade or so. The electoral process has failed to generate any impact in the minds of youth, the common people who seem to have accepted that elections cannot be fair. The blatant misuse of everything possible has reduced the credibility of the elections. Many of us seriously believe that the damages are beyond repairs.

The first reform suggested is to make it mandatory for the candidate to have 51% of votes and then only he should be deemed to be a representative of people. In case of failure repolls should be ordered.

The second suggestion is a correct appraisal of the assets of the candidate, the sources of such assets; increase in the assets if he is contesting second time should be done. In case of any anomaly the candidature should be forfeited on a permanent basis.

- The moral, ethical and criminal record of a candidate should be made public.
- In case of any irregularity at eh polling scene, such as booth capturing etc. the candidate should be banned for life.
- Defections which have been a major disease in electoral process. The antidefection bill has proved quite inadequate in controlling this menace. Any defections, in whatever percentages, should automatically result in resignation from the seat or seats. Repolls to be ordered.
- All such candidates who intentionally play with the election process should be socially out caste. All crimes pertaining to election should be treated equal to treason.

(6) Selection for government jobs should be on merit only. If the person is having the necessary qualifications, and experience, then his caste, religion, sub-caste should not matter. The person should occupy the bureaucratic chair because he or she deserves it not because he or she needs it. Human ability has nothing to do with caste or religion, as has been proved many times.

(7) The punishment to be given to proven corrupt people should be quick. All his assets should be forfeited and he should be outside the purview of any re-entry in the field. The bill to this effect should be brought

in the parliament and most importantly passed.

(8) One of the major problems in not curbing the corruption is the working of investigating and prosecuting agencies. The executive branch should have no say in such procedures. Any politician or officer found influencing an investigation should be banned for life, irrespective of his status.

(9) Registration of complaints / FIR is a very tricky business, in our country. For obvious reasons many complaints do not get even to the FIR stage. A person should be able to register his complaint on Internet subsequent to proper identification. Such a complaint should be later forwarded to the concerned authority for necessary immediate action.

(10) It should be understood by each and every citizen, that no person is bigger than it should be understood that each Indian, is a VIP in him self, who knows his rights, and more importantly his responsibility towards his nation.

There may be many more ways to fight corruption. They are all welcome. But remember unless you follow the rules laid down by you, you cannot expect any change.

Let us begin and hope for the best.

***

CHAPTER THIRTEEN

Self Evaluation Questionnaires

Self Evaluation Questionnaires

For all those persons involved in the ever-present process of growth and progress, a self evaluation is absolutely must. If you honestly answer the questions asked, you shall have your report-card on a periodic basis. The questions asked are on a broad base and it is expected of the persons attempting to answer, to read between the lines. Also expected, is that these persons should be able to redesign the question and if need be, even add a few questions of their own. After all, it is for those who want to honestly evaluate themselves.

Please treat this entire exercise as a personal evaluation and for your own improvement. You may dislike certain questions but try to be as objective as possible and check out your innermost feelings.

Very obvious that some questions shall be common to all professions.

***

There is a concept in management which is very popular these days, which is promoted very vigorously by all experts and trainers. It is called as SWOT Analysis. The letters stand for:

S-strengths

W-weaknesses

O-opportunities

T-threats

As found in all concepts when the persons start the process, they answer with respect to what is expected of them rather than what is true. The basic purpose of the SWOT is defeated and the results are not credible. The process is a great tool for analysis and self-introspection if applied in a proper way.

So, to increase the efficacy of the SWOT process it is suggested that one may have two sets of SWOTs. One can be for the public and the second can be for the self. In the first type, one can be formal and the same can be used in the interviews as more practical way. Nothing wrong in it, after all not everybody is entitled to know your inner self. Moreover, they may use it against your interests.

The second type which, I term as a Personal SWOT needs to be done more seriously and more truthfully. It would yield you better results as you would understand your self in a better way. You have to be very ruthless in assessment so that you can expect better future and growth.

The questionnaires are designed for a personal SWOT. Please approach them in utmost seriousness and you would be benefitted.

***

The professions chosen are from the cross section of society. They are –
(1) Architects (2) Advocates
(3) Bankers (4) Chartered Accountants
(5) Doctors (6) Industrialists
(7) Salesmen (8) Managers
(9) Editor (10) Professors
(11) Bureaucrats

***

(1) ARCHITECTS:

1. Are you creative? Can you remember at least 5 of your designs which you can call as creative?
2. Do you keep yourself up-to-date? In what way? Can you improve?
3. Did you win any prizes in any Design Competitions?
4. How do you see the role of regulating authorities? How often you manage them to get your things done?
5. Do you think that "53" grade cement is promoted, when it is not really needed?
6. What is the role of a Structural Consultant?
7. An architect is primarily responsible for the buildings even though he does not provide structural designs. Do you think this is right, or any modifications needed?
8. Do you have your dream project ready?
9. Are you more of a builder's architect or you having your own say in any ongoing project?

10. When was the last time you actually took measurements / or inspected sites / or rejected a bill of contractor, on grounds of quality?

11. How do you cope up with the insufficiencies, or attitudes of "Chalta Hai", generally found on construction sites?

12. If you were a client, would you select yourself as an architect? If yes why? If no why?

13. How much of ambience plays part in your designs?

14. Have you read "The Fountainhead" by Ayn Rand?

15. Are you proud about your achievements? How can you better them?

16. Are you respected by the society for your money, or for your achievements, your insistence for quality and your integrity?

17. Do you think that the architects of earlier era were smarter?

18. How often you specify usage of construction chemicals? Are you aware about them?

19. How do you design? Do you "see" first and then design or vice versa?

20. Are you a "commission man? Or a "clean man?"

***

(2) ADVOCATES:

1. Are you in this profession by choice or as a last choice?

2. Do you have faith in "Truth shall prevail?"

3. When was the last time you laughed as innocently as a child?

4. Are you a lawyer or a middleman?

5. If you are a client, would you select yourself as an advocate? If yes, why; if no why?

6. Do you keep yourself up-to-date? How do you do it?

7. Do you feel that you can find an honest and successful lawyer in today's society? When did you last see such a person?

8. What is your impression about overall functioning of the judiciary? What improvements would you want in it? What improvements would you want in it? How would you bring about them?

9. When you see that injustice has been dished out to your client what do you do? Do you know the procedures of impeachment?

10. If there was no threat of "contempt of court" how many judges you would respect for their ability?

11. When was the last time you won a case, and felt good about it?

12. What is your percentage of success? How many cases do you settle out of court?
13. What is your opinion about Indians?
14. What is the contribution of lawyers in such huge backlog of pending cases in counts?
15. "That lawyers have to wear a black coat is a signal enough for people not to approach them" comment.
16. "Because everyone else is corrupt, I have to do it." How often do you say this? Would you be able to survive in a clean situation?
17. Did you know about Telgi Stamps? What should be, now, done to avoid such a scam not to occur again? What are the other areas in your profession, where such scams can occur?
18. Is judiciary really an independent body?
19. What is civil, about civil law practice?
20. "Justice delayed is justice denied", has lost it relevance. Comment upon this

***

(3) BANKERS:

1. What business are you in?
2. What do you understand about public finance system?
3. What is your evaluation process for correct finance to a correct party?
4. What is your risk-taking capability? How often you finance to a wrong party?
5. What is your contribution to the success of your institution?
6. Do you really understand a Balance Sheet? How do you know whether it is a doctored one, or not?
7. Your senior officer is in a process of sanctioning a loan to a bad party. What do you do about it? Keep quiet or take steps to protect the interest of your bank?
8. How comfortable are you with e-commerce? How do you prevent computer frauds?
9. What are your reading habits?
10. How do you deal with unions? As a nuisance or as a helping hand?
11. How often you are late in sending the required reports? Why?
12. If you were given complete freedom, would you still follow the prevalent systems? If yes, why? If you propose some changes, why?

13. How do you react to corruption at your corporate office? Do you accept it as a part of the necessary adjustment, or you intend to fight the same?

14. Do you see solutions when you see a problem or depend heavily on your superiors for solutions?

15. What future you see for the Indian Banking Industry as compared to the International Banks?

16. What is the public perception of banks, why?

17. What is your impression about PMRY / JRY / BPL / and all such schemes floated, on a time-to-time basis?

18. Your perception about priority sector? Why it in necessary?

***

(4) CHARTERED ACCOUNTANTS:

1. As a custodian of all the money in your nation, how do you rate your performance?

2. Do you have own ready-reckoner for preventing wrong audit practices?

3. How often you sign doctored balance sheets under the garb of saving taxes?

4. Are you a regular chartered accountant? Or you are an Income Tax Practitioner?

5. Do you pay your taxes as per the rules?

6. What is your, general and specific opinion on your professional colleagues?

7. Do you think that CAG / AG / CDA / IT / are doing what they should be doing? Give reasons to support your logic.

8. Chartered Accountant is a glorified middleman, comment on this, with reasons.

9. You support corruption because you do not have any other option.

10. How many honest and successful CAs you know?

11. How do you rate success? Are you successful?

12. When somebody talks about India, national spirit, patriotism how do you react? Why?

13. As compared to the international audit systems where do you put Indian system? Can you name the country which has the best audit system, Tax recovery system?

14. What do you think about agriculture income? Do you think the present system of taxation beats the basis purpose, as it helps the wealthy to

become even wealthier?

15. Can you design a system of uniform taxation of entire country?

16. What percentage of taxes and duties are really collected? Out of the collected money what percentage is spent on development of nation?

17. If taxation is simplified will your clients pay the correct tax?

18. What is the image of your profession in the public mind? And why?

***

(5) DOCTORS

1. Do you remember Hippocratic Oath verbatim? When was the last time your reiterated it?

2. What is you contribution to the ill famous rings in your city?

3. If your parents are also Doctors, what is difference between their attitude and yours?

4. "India needs good doctors not the medical professional." Comment on this with reasons.

5. Have you recently seen any honest, successful and capable doctor? How is he different that you? Match your attributes with him.

6. These days doctors never hold a hand for pulse diagnosis? Why?

7. What sort of medical scenario you anticipate in, say 2020 AD?

8. Do you really believe that the medical council has any say in regulation of health practices in India? What should be its role and how it can become a potent force?

9. What is your opinion on present Medico Legal System? How does it hamper your practice? Can you suggest any betterment?

10. As an acknowledged second only to the God, how do you place yourself? How many miles you are away form such a status?

11. Do you really contribute to research as stated on your hospital name board? When was the last time you produced a research paper you are proud of?

12. What are the factors which contribute, to make a successful doctor? Evaluate yourself on this scale.

13. How much adept are you with the new advance machines that have come into play? Do you really understand their printouts?

14. What are your reading habits? What are your spare time activities?

15. Do you have a farm house?

16. When you prescribe a branded drug, what are the reasons for it?

17. What is your justification for the "corrupt" medical practices in India?

18. There is a tendency to undermine everything. The pharmaceutical company schemes, farm houses, under the table dealings, unnecessary diagnostic tests, false (insurance) medical tests, avoiding normal deliveries, unnecessary neonatal complications, surgeons behaving like the proverbial butcher, unhygienic conditions in ICCU / ICU and so many to the things which you know better. How do you react? Try to state reasons for each of your responses.

19. Why Government Hospitals are not what they used to be? (Say in 1970) What went wrong and when? Can you suggest any measures to rejuvenate this system?

20. As a patient would you select 'you as a doctor? If yes why? If no why?

21. What is the image of your profession in the mind of public?

22. How do you keep yourself updated?

23. Do you do the self evaluation?

24. Do you always put in your best effort?

***

(6) INDUSTRIALISTS

1. How do you relate to present day situation in our country?

2. How do you rate yourself, your unit? Why?

3. Given an unlimited finance can you plan for your success?

4. How often you compromise with quality and feel bad about it?

5. All labor problems are due to illogical government regulations? Comment on this statement with reasons.

6. Are you where you should be? If yes why, if no why?

7. Do you keep yourself updated? How?

8. What is your debtors / creditors position?

9. Do you understand ratio analysis as prevalent in accounting? How do your place your unit?

10. The original entrepreneurial temperament is long gone. Comment on this.

11. Who is responsible for the present status of small-scale industries? Why?

12. When you see success of some one else, how do you react?

13. Your evaluation on the socio-economic condition of your country, with reasons?

14. How many times you outsmarted the banker by doing what you are not supposed to do?
15. Would you prefer your son as an industrialist or as an employed person somewhere else?
16. Do you know any honest, successful and capable industrialist? What are the reasons for his success? Could you become more successful applying his success rules?
17. "No one can make money if he follows all the regulations in force" Your Comments.
18. What are you reading habits?
19. Do you understand investments?

***

(7) SALESMEN / SALES MANAGERS:

1. Are you in this profession by choice or as a last choice?
2. Do you understand the sales process?
3. Have you read Philip Kotler's book on marketing?
4. What is the public perception about your profession, why?
5. Do you have satisfied customers? Can you name at least five?
6. What makes an ideal sales person? How far or near are you from such a person?
7. When was the last time you won any award?
8. How punctual are you in writing reposts?
9. How do you deal with product complaint?
10. Do you know what NSR is? what is your NSR
11. What are your reading habits?
12. What is the difference between sales and marketing?
13. Evaluate yourself on the following:

   a. appearance
   b. presentation skills
   c. integrity
   d. dealing with competition
   e. orders ratio
   f. product knowledge
   g. outstanding position
   h. communication skills

    a. temperament
    j. new customers, new markets, new applications of existing products
    k. after sales service
  ax. N S R
  all. Relations with dealers / stockiest

14. Are you ready for a promotion? What changes would you make, and why?
15. Are you comfortable in frontline selling?
16. How can you better yourself?
17. How does your performance compare with others in your own company?
18. How do you keep your self updated?
19. Would you allow your son to be in the same profession? Why?
20. Can you name at least 5 professional achievements, on a yearly basis?

***

(8) MANAGERS:

1. Are you a manager in the true sense of the word?
2. As a profit centre, rate your performance.
3. Do you grab the credits of your juniors?
4. Are you respected for your integrity and values?
5. Do you have at least 2 job offers as on today?
6. What is your contribution to your company?
7. Do you have any training ability?
8. What are your professional achievements? Can you name at least 5 on a yearly basis?
9. What is your initiative level? How often you volunteer for new assignments?
10. Do you believe in present day management system?
11. What are your reading habits?
12. Are you professionally qualified? Such as an MBA etc. How does it help you?
13. Management is all about man management. Comment on this with reference to your own company.
14. What are your plus and minus features?
15. Comment on your –

a. attitude
b. procedural competence
c. goal setting and achieving
d. human angle towards our juniors
e. crisis management
f. promotion history
g. integrity
h. decision taking capacity
a. action plans and implementation of them

16. Industrial relations and labor unrest. How do you cope with it?
17. How often you allow, fall in quality for meeting production targets?
18. Do you have an IDOL as a manager? Why?
19. How do you rate commitment of an employee vis-à-vis his professional expertise?
20. Are you happy to be a manager?

***

9. **EDITORS:**
10. Are you in this profession by choice?
11. Do you really believe in what you write as an editor?
12. Do you have any idol? Why?
13. How committed journalism has affected India? Are you a part of it? How do you justify it?
14. "Newspapers have become a business rather than a mission." Your comments and reasons for or against the above statements.
15. What is the nuisance value of a publication? How do you cope up with it?
16. Are you satisfied with your output or you need a change?
17. Would you be remembered by people for your integrity, free and frank opinions?
18. How far or near you find yourself from Lokmanya Tilak, Acharya Atre, N. Ram or Aurn Shourie as an editor?
19. Do you have the journalistic instinct still alive in you? When was the last time you got a scoop, on your own?
20. Do you think that all awards in journalism are fixed?

21. Yellow journalism, blackmailing, poor language, laid back attitude, absence of investigation instincts, are the major diseases in present day journalism. Comment on this.
22. "The independence of press is a myth. You are as free as your owner allows you to be." Is it true?
23. What is the public perception of your profession?
24. Pen used to be mightier than the sword, it is not for today. Do you really think what you write can change at least some people?
25. What percentage of people you think read editorials, in any publication? What efforts you can suggest to improve this situation?
26. With so many undesirable persons and activities around you, how do you cope up?
27. What do you do in your free time? What are your achievements? Do you read a lot?
28. Are happy to be an editor?
29. Please evaluate yourself on following –
30. correctness of thought
31. correctness of language
32. fighting for a correct cause
33. impression of your staff about you
34. periodic advancement
35. investigative journalists

***

(10) Professors / teachers:

1. Are you in this profession by choice or by compulsion?
2. Do your students respect you for your knowledge?
3. What is the color of your notes? Are they yellow?
4. Would you employ yourself as a professor in your own college?
5. When was the last time you referred to a technical journal?
6. When was the last time you contributed by way of a research paper in any journal?
7. If the "internal marks system" is abolished would your students still respect you?
8. Are you a teacher or a Guru?
9. Do you love your students?
10. Can you remember students by their first names?

11. When was the last time, student came to your house for advice?
12. How do you keep yourself updated?
13. Do you take feedback from your students?
14. Is your effort of teaching genuine or indifferent?
15. How often you whine about the following standards in education?
16. Are you comfortable with computers, internet? Do you use them?
17. What are your achievements on a yearly basis for the last 5 years?
18. Do you really lend a helping hand to your students?
19. What is the relationship between the degree the student gets and his level of knowledge? Please comment.
20. Evaluate yourself on the following –

    a. knowledge of the subject
    b. current knowledge
    c. expression, correct language
    d. temperament
    e. results over a period of last five years
    f. private tuitions taken
    g. attendance in your classes
    h. your relationship with you colleagues
    a. enthusiasm level
    j. Your contribution, in the institute, you work for.

***

(11) BUREAUCRATS:

1. When you see a mirror do you remember "Yes Minister"?
2. You are responsible for your country's present status. How much responsibility you own for the mess in our country?
3. When was the last time you took an independent initiative and succeeded?
4. You alone cannot fight corruption; hence you become part of it. Is it true?
5. How close are you to the ground reality?
6. How near you find yourself to your idol, it you have any?
7. Bureaucrats are trained to hamper progress anywhere. Why is it so?
8. What is the public perception about you? Why?

9. The rules are quite powerful but a weak implementation has been a main factor creating a chaos this situation? What is your contribution?

10. How an ignorant elected person can dominate you?

11. Do you really think that you are delivering right goods?

12. How often you can say that you discharged your duties as per the expectation of the people?

13. With so many undesirable people and activity around you how do you cope up? Are you bitter about India?

14. Can you recount your achievements on yearly basis for the last 5 years?

15. With so much collective intelligence, cumulative capacity at hand, do you feel that your country is where it should be?

16. In any case of corruption or irregularity it is always a junior official who is punished? Why?

17. Corruption starts at the top, or the bottom. What do you think and why?

18. The will is always lacking to fight the undesirable elements, is a common impression about bureaucrats. What do you think?

19. Does your country really need such a hierarchically structured bureaucracy? Can you suggest any other model?

20. How do you rate yourself? Can you be better?

21. You could have been a part of destiny of your country but for...... please comment.

****

www.ingramcontent.com/pod-product-compliance
Lightning Source LLC
Chambersburg PA
CBHW051128160726

47997CB00018B/821